What Every Kid and Adult Should Know About Computers

Arthur Naiman

Illustrations by Rick Hackney

This book was produced by the author in collaboration with:
Guy Orcutt—cover photography and photographs of screens
Edith Allgood—interior design and production
Sharon Skolnick—cover design
Rick Hackney—cartoon illustrations
Andrew Bunnin, Suzette Pilgrim—cover models
Aptos Post Typography,
Ann Flanagan Typography—typesetting

The screen photo of Pinball Construction Set shown on the cover courtesy of Electronic Arts, 2755 Campus Drive, San Mateo, CA 94403.

Library of Congress Cataloging in Publication Data

Naiman, Arthur.
What every kid and adult should know about computers.

Summary: An introduction to the world of computers, describing what they do, how to program, where to get more information, and interesting sidelights.
1. Computers—Juvenile literature. [1. Computers] I. Title.
QA76.23.N35 1985   001.64   84-29762
ISBN 0-8104-6336-9

Printed in the United States of America

S 10 9 8 7 6 5 4 3 2 1

This book is for my big-eyed honey
Who's cute and sweet and smart and funny.
She's 29 going on 8
And I really think she's great.

Acknowledgments

In March 1983 I went to the wedding of Judi Gibian and Ken Mennenga, who—in addition to their many other virtues—are experts on the use of computers in education. Somewhere between the square dancing and the honey and garlic dip, I learned that a book like this was needed and started thinking about writing it. Many people have contributed their ideas and knowledge since then, and this is where I thank them.

Meg Holmberg helped this book in too many ways to list here; one of her greatest services was to put me in touch with Lynne Alper, Bill Finzer, and the people at EQUALS (of whom I particularly want to thank Mattye Pollard, Helen Joseph and Tim Erickson). It's always nice, when you're getting started writing a book, to run into people who can just sit down and tell you everything you need to know; it saves a lot of time on research. The people in this paragraph got me pointed in all the right directions, and cut my research time by at least 90%.

My agent, Esther Wanning, was terrific (as always); her retirement from the agenting business is a blow from which the publishing industry will probably never recover. Lila (aka Xenia) Lisanevich made a zillion different contributions to the book, everything from writing to software publishers to copy-editing the final manuscript. Brad Bunnin provided his usual crystal-clear, perfectly balanced advice.

After a seemingly endless search for designers who knew what they were doing, didn't cost too much, had the time to work on this book and, on top of all that, could get along with someone as fussy as me, I felt like a parched desert traveler dragging himself into an oasis when I finally hooked up with Edith Allgood and Sharon Skolnick. Each of them did a terrific job.

Rick Hackney also suffered from my fussiness, but always came through on incredibly short notice. Guy Orcutt supplemented his excellent photographs with some very helpful and perceptive design suggestions. Suzette Pilgrim and Andrew Bunnin worked hard for their money, and added a lot to the cover of the book.

Les Purificacion is a great editor who isn't afraid to fight for what is right. It was a real pleasure to deal with someone as sensible, as intelligent and as dedicated to producing a quality book as Les is. Jim Bernard made several astute suggestions concerning the cover design. Eric Jungerman did some early design work and clarified a number of production issues.

Even though I was a complete stranger to her, Phyllis Dolhinow was kind enough to read the first chapter and suggest a number of changes. I also want to thank John Kert and Vincent Sarich for answering my questions when I called them up out of the blue.

Susan Rawlins provided me with an instant audience, by having a dozen of her high-school students read a draft of part of the book. Thanks to her, I was able to find the right tone of voice much more quickly, and with a lot less floundering than would otherwise have been the case.

Writing a book like this is very much a communal, collaborative effort. The following people read drafts of various parts of the book, supplied crucial bits of information, gave me their opinions on all sorts of different questions, and/or supported me in many other ways:

Gloria Zarifa, Ira Rosenberg, Steve Warner, Michael Bradley, Katie Turner, Julie Sickert, Gloria Polanski, Ron Lichty (who's still batting a thousand—seven acknowledgments in seven books), Laurie Capitelli, Matthew and Sarah Capitelli, Chris Carpenter, Rita Gibian, Albert and Nettie Naiman, Don Kenney, Sherri Fraser, Ed Kelly, Eileen Callahan, Mike McGrath, Nancy Ragle, Gar Smith, Vic Fischer, Cheryl Nichols, Mary Mackey, Pete Lundstrom, Rose Slais, Roz Kulick, Sandy Van Broek, Sanji Rosenberg, Ishvi Aum, Stew Albert, Judy and Jessica Clavir Albert, Yvette Manson, Toby Klayman, Susan Strasburger, Ted Friedman, Michael Isador, Court Miller, Madalyn Pilgrim, Debra Dadd, David Socholitzsky, Jane Margold, Meg Gawler, Vince Stubbs, Eric Angress, Terra Candage, Nevin Pfaltzgraff and Nancy Shine.

Contents

Introduction

There's a saying that the easier a book is to write, the harder it is to read. I've worked very hard to make this book a pleasure to read.

I've aimed the writing at teenagers and bright 8- to 12-year-olds, and also at adults who feel intimidated by computers (a real pity, since computers are a lot of fun, and not even hard to understand). I talk about all the main ways you can enjoy computers, but I don't try to cover every single thing you can do with them.

If you've already been exposed to computers in school, you may have been turned off to them. Teachers who don't understand the real power of computers try using them to do things like teach you *multiplication tables!* That's a little like using a car to drive from the living room to the dining room—when where you really want to go is the beach.

This book is pro-kids and anti-boredom. I believe that if you don't like doing something, it's probably not worth doing. Computers are *very* powerful tools. Like any powerful tool, they are a lot of fun to use. If this book does one thing, I hope it convinces you of that.

The first chapter talks about what computers do, and about a lot of other things too— like how big dolphins' and gorillas' brains are, or why we walk on two legs instead of on four like most animals.

The second chapter tells you how computers work. In his book *Cat's Cradle*—which is great, by the way—Kurt Vonnegut says that any scientist who can't explain his work to an eight-year-old is a phony. I'm not a scientist, but if I couldn't explain computers to an eight-year-old, I'd certainly have no business writing this book.

Then I begin telling you all the different things you can do with a computer (I'll give you the details at the end of Chapter 1).

If you want to know what all the computer terms mean, you should read the book straight through, each chapter in order, since I define them the first time I mention them. I also boldface them (**boldfacing looks like this**). That's so it's easy for you to find them later, and also so you won't feel like a dope when you run across a word you've never seen before (if it's boldfaced, you're not *supposed* to know what it means).

But even if you skip around, you can still look up a term you don't know in the index (I boldface the page number where the definition is).

Well, that's enough of an introduction; nobody reads the introduction anyway.

Chapter   1

What Computers Do and Why There's Any Point in Learning about Them

Right from the beginning, I want you to know that this book isn't going to try to cram you full of information somebody says you *should learn*. The only reason anything is included here is that I thought you'd enjoy reading about it. Fortunately, it wasn't hard to find interesting things to say about computers, since they're just about the most fascinating machines that have ever been invented.

Even though this book is about computers, I don't begin talking about them until the end of this chapter. That's because the best way to tell you about computers is to first discuss human beings— what we're like and how we got to be the way we are today. So don't worry if I seem to be rambling around a bit in this chapter; we'll get to computers soon enough, and then we'll spend the rest of the book on them.

If you woke up one morning and found yourself all alone, naked, in the middle of a forest, there are a number of things you could do. If you wanted to go somewhere, you could walk or run. If you wanted to see something, you could turn your eyes toward it and look at it. If you wanted to get away

naked in the middle of a forest

from something that was chasing you, you could climb a tree (and hope that it couldn't).

But if you look at human beings just in terms of these natural abilities of ours, we're one of the least impressive animals around. We're incredibly slow for our size—even a small dog can outrun us. Our eyes aren't too bad, but almost any bird has better ones. We're OK at climbing trees, since our ancestors did a lot of that, but we're still nowhere near as good at it as squirrels.

almost any bird has better eyes

Even though most of our physical abilities are just fair (and a lot of them are really poor), we've been able to build so many roads and cities and shopping malls and golf courses that we've just about forced every other kind of animal off the face of the earth (except for the ones we raise for our own purposes, like cattle and sheep and horses).

How have we managed to do that? Well, it's all the result of the only two pieces of natural equipment we have that really are outstanding— our hands and our brains. Many of our other abilities have been skipped over so that our hands and our brains could develop. One good example is the fact that we walk (and run) on two legs.

running on two legs
is clumsy and slow

Running on two legs is clumsy and slow; that's why almost all of the fastest-running animals use four legs. Then why do we do it? What advantage does it give us that makes up for the loss of speed? Well, basically, we walk on two legs to free up our hands so we can carry things.

*we walk on two legs to free up
our hands so we can carry things*

The experts don't all agree on what we originally used our hands to carry when we first came down from the trees millions of years ago; maybe it was food we were bringing back to the children in camp, maybe rocks to throw at game (animals we wanted to eat) or at predators (animals that wanted to eat us).

But whatever our hands first carried, eventually we started using them to make tools. Tools are the secret to our success, because tools help us overcome our physical weaknesses.

All tools improve on one or another of our natural abilities. For example, we can break a stick with our hands—or, if it's too thick for that, by stepping on it. But a hatchet or an ax makes the job much easier, and allows us to cut sticks we couldn't dream of breaking otherwise.

Some tools help us do a combination of things.

For example, the tool you see below can be used to get a banana down from a tree without climbing (mostly it's used to get boxes down from high shelves).

Not every tool is the kind you can buy in a hardware store. Cars, trains and airplanes are all tools, because they improve on our natural ability to walk. So are shoes—they help us run through the jungle without scuffing up our feet.

shoes help us run through the jungle without scuffing up our feet

Tools don't even have to be machines. For example, horses are tools that improve on our natural ability to walk, because we can tame them and ride them. And many people say that the most important tool of all is language—our ability to talk to each other. (If you don't see how language is a tool, try going through just one day of your life without saying a single word to anybody.)

our ability to tame horses

The first tools human beings ever made were probably pointed sticks used for digging up food, or sharp chipped stones used for cutting up food. Then came the "stone ax"–a chipped stone tied onto a stick. Making even primitive tools like these required good hands that could do complicated, precise things.

But good hands are worthless if you don't know what to do with them—just as beautiful handwriting is worthless if you don't know what to write. And inventing and then making even a simple tool like a stone ax put a big demand on the human brain (which started out pretty small).

The ape women and men who could figure out how to make better digging sticks and stone axes were able to get more food than other tribes, and so their population increased faster. When there were fights over a particular hunting ground or watering hole, the smarter tribe would usually win them, because it had better tools to fight with. In this way, there got to be more and more smart ape people and fewer and fewer dumb ones.

Today, after millions of years of making tools, our brains are a lot larger than they used to be, but they're still not the biggest around. Some big animals—like elephants—have brains that weigh more than ours. But they also have bodies that weigh more than ours. And while elephants are pretty smart, nobody thinks they're smarter than us.

Just the size of an animal's brain is not a sure indication of how smart it is. A better way to get some idea of that is to figure out how many pounds of brain an animal has for each pound of its whole body.

This is still not very dependable. For example, there's absolutely no connection between what an individual human being's brain weighs and how smart s/he is. Albert Einstein, one of the smartest people who ever lived, had a very small brain (it was weighed and studied after he died). But when you compare different *kinds* of animals, how much brain each one has for every pound of body gives you some kind of rough idea of how smart each one is.

The average human brain weighs around three pounds. The average human body weighs around 120 pounds. (Whenever I talk about brain weights and body weights, I'm talking about adults. If 120 pounds seems light, remember that most of us are

Almost 1 lb.

3/4 lb.

450 lbs.

100 lbs.

Asian and most of us are women.) So we have about 40 pounds of body weight for every pound of brain.

Now let's compare our two closest animal relatives, chimpanzees and gorillas. The average chimpanzee brain weighs around ¾ of a pound, and the average chimpanzee weighs around 100 pounds. So chimpanzees have about 135 pounds of body weight for every pound of brain—much less brain to go around than we do.

The gorilla does even worse. Gorilla brains average a little less than a pound, but gorillas weigh an average of about 450 pounds; they have about 480 pounds of body weight for every pound of brain.

It's not that chimpanzees and gorillas are stupid;

3 lbs.

120 lbs.

in fact, they're just about the smartest animals there are. Cows have about 1125 pounds of body for every pound of brain. Grizzly bears have 600 pounds of body for every pound of brain. And even elephants—with their big ten-pound brains—still have about 650 pounds of body for every pound of brain.

Not only do we humans have more brain per pound of body weight, we also have a *better brain*. The part that actually does the thinking (as opposed to just controlling different parts of the body) takes up much more of our brain than it does in any other kind of animal—except for some dolphins.

Bottlenose dolphins, for example, have brains that weigh about 3½ pounds in bodies that weigh

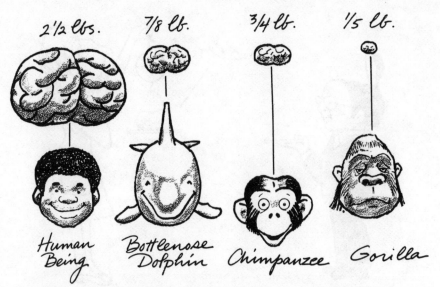

2½ lbs.   7/8 lb.   3/4 lb.   1/5 lb.

Human Being   Bottlenose Dolphin   Chimpanzee   Gorilla

how much brain different animals have

about 400 pounds; this gives them 115 pounds of body weight for each pound of brain. But the thinking part of their brains is 40% larger than ours. That's one reason why some people say dolphins are smarter than we are. (Two other reasons: they don't wage war and they don't watch television.)

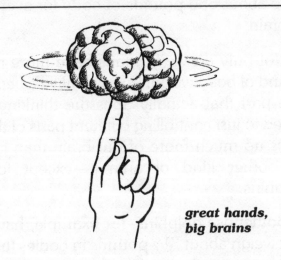

great hands, big brains

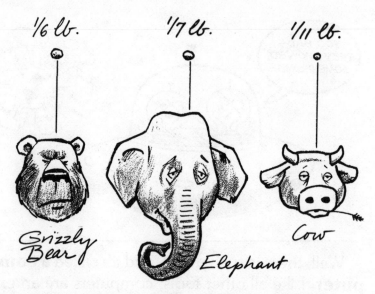

¹/₆ lb.　　¹/₇ lb.　　¹/₁₁ lb.

Grizzly Bear　　Elephant　　Cow

for every 100 pounds of body weight

To sum up—we human beings have survived on this planet (where so many other kinds of animals are dying out) basically because we have:

- great hands
- big brains.

We developed such big brains to help our hands make better and better tools that do more and more things.

Unfortunately, there's a limit to what brains even as big as ours can do; this is obvious when you stop to realize that we may soon use nuclear weapons to turn ourselves (and everything else in the world) into a lot of radioactive guacamole. So it would really be great if we could make a tool that helps our brain, a tool that helps us think better.

Well, there is such a tool, and it's called a **computer.** Like all other tools, computers are an extension of one of our natural abilities (thinking, in this case). With computers, we can have brains that weigh more than our whole bodies do, even though it takes many pounds of computer to equal one pound of brain. (Whether they'll help us not blow ourselves up is another story.)

Now, I have to say right away that, so far at least, computers can't really *think*. What they do is help us think—in just the same way that a telescope helps us see, although it can't see by itself. But some day in the not-too-distant future, computers will actually be able to think.

Because computers are extensions of our brains, rather than of some other part of our bodies, they have many special qualities. For one thing, they're very versatile. ("Versatile" means "able to do a lot of different things." So if you can sing, act and tap-dance, you're versatile. If you can play the piano too, you're even more versatile.)

computers are versatile

Our brains are the most versatile parts of our bodies, because we can use them to think about, to imagine, many more things than we could ever make with our hands or travel to with our feet or see with our eyes. Since computers help the brain, it's no surprise that they're also more versatile than any other tool that has ever been invented.

Big computers can do things like predict the weather, design buildings, and do very complicated arithmetic. Some of the new "supercomputers" can do almost a hundred *million* additions or subtractions *every second*.

But computers can also help you do everyday things better. Here are a few of the ways you can have fun with them:

Drawing

Most computers can't talk, so they communicate with you on a screen like the one on a TV set. You can make all kinds of pictures on the screen. The computer will remember them for you and draw them again on the screen whenever you say, or will make permanent copies of them on paper.

Some computers will even take a picture you've drawn and make it bigger or smaller, or stretch it wider or taller the way a mirror in a fun house does. Chapter 3 tells you about using computers to draw.

Making music

A lot of the new music you hear is actually played on computers (or on electronic musical instruments called "synthesizers" which have computers in them). When you write a piece of music

on a computer (and you can do that within five minutes of sitting down at the keyboard), the computer memorizes it and will repeat it for you whenever you want.

You can also tell the computer to make it twice as fast, or twice as slow, or raise or lower the pitch, or make one particular note twice as long, or take out these three notes here, or repeat the pattern there—and the computer will do it automatically. See Chapter 4 for more details.

Writing

If you're one of those people who hates to write something down because you're afraid that the first thing you put down on paper will sound stupid, computers are for you. They make it so easy to change things that you never have to worry about the first thing you write—since you can rewrite it a dozen times before it ever goes onto paper.

Computers will also automatically check your spelling, teach you how to touch-type (while destroying alien spacecraft), and help you write stories that have many different endings. Chapter 5 tells you more about writing on computers.

Playing games

This is one use of computers you probably already know about. All those video games like Pac Man and Donkey Kong and Asteroids are basically computers, whether they're the little ones you hook up to your TV or the big arcade machines you have to feed quarters to. Chapter 6 tells you about some of the more interesting games you can play on a computer, ones you probably don't know about.

Other things you can do on a computer

Chapter 7 covers everything from making birthday cards, banners and posters to talking to other computers over the phone lines.

Really incredible stuff

Of all the things computers do well, they're probably best at pretending they're something else. Programs that let a computer do this are called **simulations.** Chapter 8 describes software that lets you use the computer screen to:

- build your own working pinball machines
- travel through the body's bloodstream and

fight off actual germs with the same drugs doctors use to fight them (a doctor helped write this program, and it's used to train medical students)

- build robots and use them to escape from a city completely populated by other robots (you're the only human being there)

- fly a plane out of Chicago, New York, Boston, Los Angeles or Seattle. This program comes complete with realistic maps that show all the airports in these areas, and on the screen are all the dials and gauges you find in the cockpit of an actual plane (all the important ones, anyway). Once you get good at flying, the program lets you engage in a dogfight, in a real WWI plane, against other WWI planes.

Programming

There are lots of other things computers can do, and programming is the way you teach computers to do them. Chapter 9 talks about how to program a computer (which is easier than it sounds).

In all those chapters, I describe a few programs in detail, so you get some idea of the kinds of things you can do, and then I mention some other software that's also good. The programs I use as examples aren't necessarily the best there are (although often they are), and there may be some wonderful software out there that I don't even mention. But if I do mention a program, either I've tried it and liked it, or it's been recommended to me by people whose judgment I respect.

Chapter 10 tells you which are the best computers to buy, and what to look for when buying software. Chapter 11 tells you how to convince parents and teachers to buy the right stuff, instead of wasting their money on junk. Chapter 12 tells you where you can find out more about computers, and how to find one to use for free if you can't afford to buy one.

Then comes the appendix. The first time I mention a piece of software or hardware in the book, I give the name of the publisher or manufacturer in parentheses after it; the appendix lists the addresses and phone numbers of all these companies.

Finally, there's a *very* complete index. I hate indexes you can't find things in, so when I made this one, I put *everything* in it.

That's what you can expect from Chapter 3 on. But before I get into what computers can do, it makes sense to spend a little time explaining how they work. That's what Chapter 2 does.

Chapter 2

How Computers Work

Math can be a pretty interesting subject, if your school is any good at teaching it. But plain old arithmetic—adding, subtracting, multiplying and dividing—is too boring for any human being to really enjoy. So people have always looked for machines to do their arithmetic for them. These machines are called **calculators.**

One of the most ancient kinds of calculator is the **abacus**. It uses beads on wires and is thousands of years old. If you're lucky, you may be able to find a Chinese business that still uses

an abacus

an abacus, so you can see how fast an expert can do arithmetic with you. In Japanese schools today, children learn to use the abacus as a regular part of their studies, and even have contests, with prizes, to see who's the fastest on it.

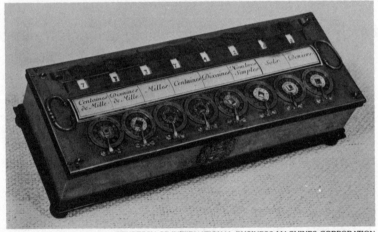

Pascal's calculator

The first modern calculator was invented by the French mathematical genius Blaise Pascal in 1642, when he was only 19 years old (the computer language Pascal is name after him). Pascal's calculator was really just an adding machine—it couldn't multiply or divide—but all of today's electronic calculators are direct descendants of it.

Useful as calculators are, their abilities are limited. They can only do what they've been wired to do; you can't teach them to do new things. Calculators you *can* teach to do new things are called . . . **computers,** and they do a whole lot more than just calculate.

The first computer—called the "analytical engine"–was designed around 1850 by an Englishman named Charles Babbage, who also invented the speedometer, the skeleton key and the cowcatcher that goes on the front of locomotives.

One of the people who worked with Babbage was Ada Lovelace, a brilliant mathematician who is often called the first computer programmer; the computer language Ada is named after her. Because she lived in Victorian times—when women weren't supposed to be able to think as well as men—she couldn't even sign her name to her writings about the computer. Back then, women novelists hid their identities too; for example, Mary Ann Evans called herself George Eliot, and Aurore Dupin called herself George Sand.

Charles Babbage

Lucasian Professor of Mathematics in the University of Cambridge

Engraved by Roffe, by permission from an original Family Painting

Charles Babbage (1792–1871)

Ada Lovelace (1815–52)

As you can see from their pictures, Babbage and Lovelace weren't just geniuses—they were also cute. (I have to confess that I have a bit of a crush on Ada Lovelace—even though she's too old for me.)

Babbage's computer was mechanical, but all computers today are electronic (I'll say more later about the difference between them). The first electronic computer was completed in 1943. It was called ENIAC, which stands for "electronic numerical integrator and calculator." As you can see, ENIAC was slightly larger than today's computers—not exactly a pocket model.

ENIAC, the first electronic computer (1943)

OK, that's enough history. Now let's move on to how computers— these calculators you can teach new tricks—actually work.

Almost all computers operate in the same basic way:

1. they reduce everything to numbers;

2. they use these numbers to make up codes;

3. they use these codes to represent words, musical notes, shapes on the screen, or just about anything else.

So to understand computers, it helps to understand a little about codes. Morse code is one you're probably familiar with; it's used to send messages over telegraph wires. Morse code reduces all the letters of the alphabet to different patterns of dots and dashes. "A" becomes a dot followed by a dash; "B" becomes a dash followed by three dots; "SOS" becomes dot dot dot, dash dash dash, dot dot dot; and so on.

Codes like this can be used in a lot of other ways. For example, if you were in a prison cell and wanted to communicate with someone on the the other side of a wall, you could use a code to tap out messages. The code people often use in such situations is A = one tap, B = two taps, and so on up to 26 taps for Z.

Or let's say that from your room you can see the window of a friend who lives nearby, and your parents think you use the phone too much. You could communicate by turning the lights of your room on and off in some kind of pattern. For example, off on off on might mean, "Come on over"; off on (pause) off might mean, "I wish I could, but I have to stay home and finish my homework."

Almost all computers are made up of lots of little switches that are basically like an ordinary light switch, and the codes they use are similar to the three I've just described. For example, a computer might use eight of its little switches to make up a code for the letters of the alphabet, the numbers and other symbols. When those eight switches read off on off off off off off on, the computer would recognize that as a capital A; when they read off on on off off off off on, it would recognize a small a; and so on.

Computers reduce *everything* they do to a pattern of switches that are on or off. So you communicate with a computer by telling it which switches to throw, and it communicates with you by throwing a certain pattern of switches.

To get a mental picture of how computers think, imagine a huge building with, say, half a million windows. The lights in these windows are constantly flashing on and off. Computers can throw those switches much, much faster than you can; even a little home computer throws its switches not hundreds, not thousands, but *millions* of times a *second*. So try to imagine the lights in those 500,000 windows going on and off at that speed.

It would all look like one big blur, right? That's just how it is with a computer. It works so fast you can't see what it's doing; you only see the results. This is nice because it means you don't have to bother with numbers or switch-throwing or any of that. The computer takes care of all the calculations for you.

Actually, our brains work basically the same way computers do—like computers, they're simply collections of lots and lots of little switches. The difference is that brains have many more switches than computers do—so many, in fact, that nobody has ever really counted them.

There are other differences in how computers and brains work. But there's enough similarity between the two that inventing and improving computers has taught us a lot about our brains.

It would be pretty clumsy to have to keep writing "on" and "off" to tell the computer which switches to throw, so computer people use **binary numbers**. In binary numbers, "on" becomes a 1 and "off" becomes a 0 (a zero). A little while back I gave a code for the capital letter A—off on off off off off off on; in binary, this would be 01000001, and a small a—off on on off off off off on—would be 01100001.

I don't want to go into a whole big thing about binary numbers, because you don't need to understand them to use a computer, but I will say a little about how binary numbers translate into the regular, decimal numbers we use every day.

Zero in binary numbers is equal to zero in decimal numbers, and 1 is equal to 1. Then things get funny. We've used up 0 and 1 and we don't have any other numbers available (since binary uses only 0 and 1)—so 2 in decimal becomes 10 in binary, 3 becomes 11, and 4 becomes 100. (If you know anything about New Math, you can see that "binary" is just another name for "base two.")

The chart below lists the binary numbers up to fifteen, with the regular decimal numbers on the left:

0 = 0	4 = 100	8 = 1000	12 = 1100
1 = 1	5 = 101	9 = 1001	13 = 1101
2 = 10	6 = 110	10 = 1010	14 = 1110
3 = 11	7 = 111	11 = 1011	15 = 1111

As you can see, binary numbers take up more room than decimal numbers. For example, eight only requires one number—8—in decimal, but four numbers—1000—in binary. The advantage of binary numbers is that they tell computers *directly* which switches to throw (in the case of eight, on off off off); they don't have to be translated before the computer can understand them.

Each binary 1 or 0 is called a **bit** (which stands for "*binary* dig*it*"). When you put eight bits together—to make the code for a letter, for example—you have a **byte.** A thousand—or, more usually, 1024—bytes is called a **kilobyte**; usually this is abbreviated **Kbyte** or simply **K**.

Almost all computers today can remember at least 16K of information at one time—that is, slightly more than 16,000 letters. This is equal to about 2500 or 3000 words. Some personal computers can remember over 1000K at one time—more than a million letters, or about 175,000 words. And there are giant computers that can remember millions of words at one time.

Computers reduce writing to numbers by making up a code for each letter; they reduce pictures to numbers by making them up out of dots and assigning a number to each dot (and to each blank space).

If you look at a black-and-white television screen from just a couple of inches away, you can see that the picture is made up of thousands of little dots. Each one of these little dots is light or dark, just as each of the windows in the building we talked about is either lit or not.

From close up, the dots on your TV screen are meaningless, but seen from a few feet away, they make up an understandable picture. A computer creates a picture in the same way, with a pattern of dots.

Some computers have **bit-mapped displays**; this means they have a switch permanently assigned to *every* little dot of their screens. When that switch is on, the dot on the screen is lit up; when that switch is off, the dot is dark. On other computers, the switches aren't permanently assigned, but they still control which dots light up.

As always, binary numbers tell the computer which switches to throw. To see how that can make up a picture, hold the drawing below at arm's length. To make the picture clearer, I've filled in the zeros. The detail isn't very good, of course, but that can be fixed simply by using more 1's and 0's.

```
1111111111111111111111111111111
111111●●●●●●●●●●●●●●●●●●●●111111
11111●111111111111111111●11111
11111●11●●●●●●11●●●●●●11●11111
11111●1111111111111111111●11111
11111●1111●●●1111●●●1111●11111
11111●1111●●●1111●●●1111●11111
11111●11111111●11111111●11111
11111●11111111●11111111●11111
11111●11111111●11111111●11111
11111●111111●●●●●111111●11111
11111●111●11111111●111●11111
11111●1111●●●●●●●●1111●11111
11111●11111111111111111●11111
111111●●●●●●●●●●●●●●●●●●●●111111
1111111111111111111111111111111
```

Pictures in magazines and newspapers—comic strips, for example—are made up out of dots the same way. Look at any printed picture under a microscope—30 power is perfect—and you'll see the dots (this won't work for actual photographs, like snapshots).

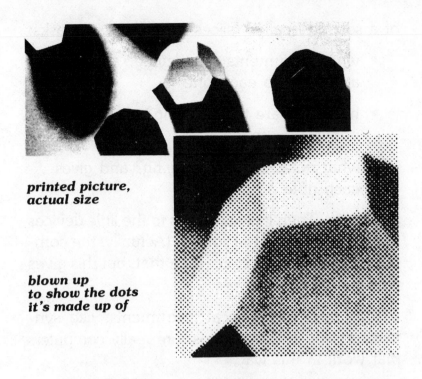

*printed picture,
actual size*

*blown up
to show the dots
it's made up of*

Computers can also reduce music to binary numbers. In fact, that's just how digital recordings are made. **Digital** means "made up of numbers." Just about all computers are digital.

To understand how computers can make music digital, consider the difference between a regular watch and a digital watch. The regular watch doesn't break time down into little pieces; its hands just spin smoothly around the dial. But a digital watch breaks each minute into 60 seconds and displays each second as a number.

Computers do the same thing with music, but they divide each second of the music into thousands of parts. For each of these little parts of a second—called "slices"—the computer asks:

- what instruments are playing? and assigns a number to each one

- how loud are they playing? and assigns a number for that

- what notes are they playing? and gives each note a number

and so on. Then it gives orders to the little devices that actually make the sound. (Actually, the computer is much more exact than that, but this gives you the idea.)

Most modern musical instruments, like synthesizers and electric pianos, are really computers that work in this way.

Now that you have an idea of how computers work, it's time to talk about the actual equipment—called **hardware**—that makes up a computer system. (Don't expect to remember every word of this explanation. Just get a general understanding and refer back to it if you forget what a word means.)

The first and most important piece of equipment is, of course, the computer itself. It has two main parts. One is called the CPU (for "central processing unit"). That's where the computer plays with the numbers that are behind everything it does.

The second part is called **memory**, or **RAM**. ("RAM" stands for "random access memory," but

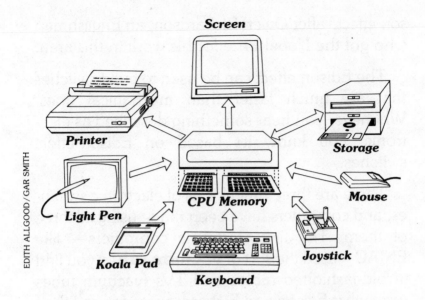

the basic parts of a computer system

don't worry about what that means.) RAM is where the computer stores the results of its calculations—which happen so fast that if it didn't store them, you'd never even see them go by.

Both the CPU and memory are made up of switches. Back in the days of Babbage's "analytical engine," these were actual mechanical switches, like light switches on the wall. But today they're always **electronic**. A while back I said I'd explain the difference, so here goes:

If you heat a piece of a certain kind of metal in a vacuum (a place where there's no air or anything else), electricity will jump from it to another piece of metal. This is called the "Edison effect," after Thomas Edison, who was one of the first people to experiment with it, or the "Richardson effect," after Owen Richardson, an Englishman who got the Nobel Prize for his work in this area.

The Edison effect can be used to build switches that are much faster than mechanical ones. Whenever you hear something described as electronic, you know it's based on Edison-effect switches.

There are three main kinds of electronic switches, and computers have been made using all three of them. The first electronic computers— like ENIAC—used the sort of **vacuum tubes** you find in old-fashioned radios and TVs (vacuum tubes were what Edison and Richardson performed their experiments on).

The next generation of computers used **transistors**, like the ones in portable radios. Transistors can create the Edison effect without needing a glass tube with a vacuum inside of it. They take up much less space, and generate much less heat, than vacuum tubes.

Today's computers use a third kind of electronic switch—the **chip**. A chip is a little square a quarter of an inch or so across—about the size of a baby's fingernail. As many as half a million switches can be squeezed onto a single chip; ten thousand or twenty thousand is common.

It would take me the rest of the book to explain the process used to get all these switches into such a little space. Basically, the electrical circuits and switches are printed onto a piece of **silicon**—

which is what sand and glass are mostly made of. The printing is very, very small.

The pictures below show what chips look like at different magnifications. You can see all the little circuits that connect the switches. Because chips are made up of a whole lot of circuits put together, they're also called **integrated circuits—ICs** for short.

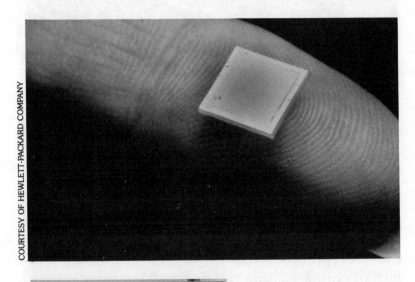

COURTESY OF HEWLETT-PACKARD COMPANY

▲
tiny chips like this one lie at the heart of all modern computers

COURTESY OF HEWLETT-PACKARD COMPANY

◄
a chip, greatly magnified to show the circuits in it

a chip in front of a few of the transistors it replaces

It's because chips have gotten so small that computers have gotten so small. You can buy a computer today that weighs a couple of pounds and costs a couple of hundred dollars that's smarter than the most powerful computer in the world twenty or thirty years ago. And that old computer filled rooms, weighed tons, and cost a fortune.

Chips are usually put inside of **DIPs**—"dual in-line packages"—which are then plugged into **boards** (also called **cards**). DIPs have two rows of legs, or "pins," and look like little caterpillars or centipedes. The pins connect the circuits on the chip with the circuits on the board. The board plugs

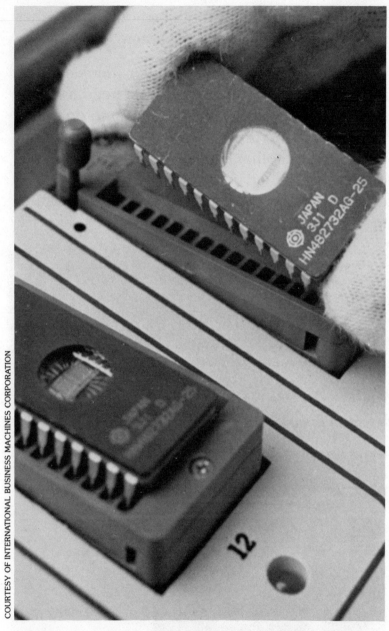

a DIP—the package most chips are placed in before they go into a computer (these DIPs have no covers, allowing you to see where the chips sit inside them)

into the computer and that's how all the switches in a computer get linked together.

OK—we've got the computer thinking and remembering its thoughts; now we need a way to communicate with it. The usual way to do that is with a **keyboard** pretty much like the one on a typewriter, but other things—like **joysticks**—can be used too. When you hit a key on the keyboard, or move a joystick, a code travels over a wire to the computer and throws some switches inside of it.

a typical computer keyboard

◀ *a joystick*

Now that we've got a way to talk to the computer, we need a way for it to talk to us. This is done on a screen like the one on a TV; in fact, you can even use your regular TV (although a special **monitor**, designed to work with computers, is easier on your eyes).

It's also nice if the computer can put what it wants to say on paper, so you can make a copy of it to take away with you or to send to someone else. The machine that does that is called a

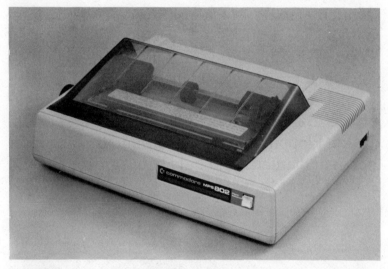

a printer

printer. A printer is sort of like a typewriter, but it's much faster and usually doesn't have a keyboard (the computer talks to it over a wire).

On almost any computer, the memory goes blank when you turn it off. So you need some way to keep a record of what you've put into the computer and what it's figured out for you. The machines that do this are called **storage devices**. (A **device** is any piece of hardware that does one specific job—in this case, it stores information.)

A cassette recorder is one thing you can use as a storage device; it stores the information as a series of sounds. Unfortunately, cassette recorders are slow and cassettes aren't very reliable. **Floppy disks** are much better.

Floppies are made of the same sort of stuff recording tape is, stuck inside a cardboard jacket that looks sort of like a 45 record. They're called "floppies" because you can bend them—although you ruin them if you bend them too much. Officially, they're called **diskettes** or **flexible diskettes**. But everybody I know just calls them **disks**. Floppies range from around three to eight inches in diameter and hold between 10,000 and 200,000 words.

a floppy disk drive built into the side of the Apple IIc

The machine that puts information onto floppy disks—and gets information back from them—is called a **floppy disk drive**. There are also **hard disk drives**. Hard disks hold more information than floppy disks—millions of words—and they get to it faster, but they also cost a lot more. Both floppy and hard disk drives store information magnetically, the same way sound is recorded on tape.

When you take information from memory and put it on a disk, that's called **saving**. When you take information from a disk and put it into memory, that's called **loading**. Each individual chunk of information you store on a disk is called a **file**.

The computer, screen, keyboard, storage device and printer don't all have to be separate pieces of equipment. Any or all of them can be combined.

an IBM Personal Computer
(the Apple II and Commodore computers are shown in Chapter 10)

a Kaypro portable computer

For example, on an Apple II or a Commodore, the keyboard and the computer are one piece and the screen is separate; on an IBM Personal Computer, the computer and the disk drives come as one piece but the keyboard and screen are separate; on a Kaypro, the computer, disk drives and screen are all combined and the keyboard latches on to them.

That pretty much covers the hardware, but hardware won't do you any good without **programs**—the instructions that tell the computer what to do. Also called **software**, these programs are basically just long lists of binary numbers that tell the computer which switches to throw. Writing software is called **programming** and you use **programming languages** to do it.

"Software" and "programs" mean exactly the same thing, by the way; the only difference is how you use them (in other words, you can't say things like "three software" or "too much programs"). Some ads now talk about "software programs." The people who wrote those ads must have been trained in the Department of Redundancy Department, since all programs are software, and all software is made up of programs.)

Software usually comes to you on a floppy disk, but sometimes it comes in a DIP, as a kind of hard-to-change memory called **ROM** ("read-only memory"). Games, which are a special kind of software, often come on tapes or cartridges. You can also write programs yourself (see Chapter 9 for more about that).

Well, that should tell you enough to make the rest of the book understandable. There's plenty to read if you want to know more about how computers work, but for most people, the fun of computers is using them, not building or fixing them. So let's get on to some of the great things you can do with them.

Chapter 3

Drawing on a Computer

Programs that let you make pictures on a computer are called **graphics** software. Before I started doing research for this book, I was used to the incredible graphics programs that run on expensive computers like the Lisa and the Macintosh. I didn't expect graphics software aimed at kids, which costs a fraction as much, to really compare. But I was amazed at how close the kids' software comes. In some ways, it's even better.

I'll describe some of that software in a moment. But before I do, I need to talk a little about the basics:

Almost every graphics program puts a mark—a cross or a dot or some other symbol—up on the screen; this is called a **cursor**. When you move the cursor, it draws a line, just as a pencil does when it moves across a sheet of paper (that's just one of the things it can do). You can make the cursor fatter, too, more like a brush, so that it makes a thicker line. But thick or thin, the first question is—how do you tell the computer where you want to move the cursor?

Input devices

You can do it with any one of a number of different **input devices** (they're called that because you use them to *put* information *in* the computer). The basic input device is a keyboard.

Some computer keyboards have keys labelled

COURTESY OF APPLE COMPUTER, INC.

the arrow keys on an Apple IIc keyboard (arrow keys are more convenient if arranged in a diamond)

with arrows pointing in all four directions; these **arrow keys** are easiest to use if they're arranged in a diamond, with the up arrow key on top, the down arrow key on the bottom, and so on.

If your keyboard doesn't have arrow keys, most graphics programs will give you other keys—also arranged in a diamond—to substitute for them. For example, on the standard keyboard, the keys for I, J, K and M are arranged like this:

$$I$$
$$J \quad \quad K$$
$$M$$

So a graphics program might make I the up arrow key, J the left arrow key, K the right arrow key and M the down arrow key. To tell the computer that you want to move the cursor, not type the letter on the key, you hold down another, special key at the same time. Usually this key has the word "CONTROL" written on it and is called the **control key**.

A **character** is any letter, number or symbol. So a command you give by hitting the control key and a character key at the same time is called a **control character**. For example, you might ask, "What's the control character for moving the cursor to the right?" And your friend might answer, "Control-K."

Whether you use arrow keys or control characters to move the cursor around, the way you're drawing on the screen is very different from the way you normally draw with a pen or a pencil. Since you have much more experience drawing that way, you have more control and can do better detail work. So it would be nice if you could draw on a computer more or less the same way.

You can come closer to that by using a joystick (if you've forgotten what a joystick looks like, there's a picture of one near the end of Chapter 2). To move the cursor, you just push the joystick in the direction you want it to go.

Even closer to a pencil is something called a **mouse**. A mouse is a small box with one or more buttons on top and a cord attaching it to the computer. You move the cursor by rolling the mouse around on the table. This is better than the joystick because you're actually moving your hand around, the way you do when you draw on paper. But it's still not quite the same thing. (Another problem with the mouse is that some **machines**—that's slang for "computers"—can't use it.)

a mouse

So what's the solution? The solution—in my humble opinion—is something like the **Koala Pad** (made by Koala Technologies). This is a...er...pad...uh...just look at the picture. You use a plastic **stylus** (like a pencil without the lead) to draw on the four-inch-square black area (the whole pad is about 6″ by 8″).

Whatever you draw with the stylus, the cursor copies on the screen (except that the cursor moves farther than the stylus does, since the screen is more than four inches across). After you use a Koala Pad for a while, it starts to feel like you're actually drawing on the screen. You don't even have to use the stylus; you can just use your finger. In fact, so many people use their fingers, that's what Koala shows in some of their official pictures (like the one below).

a Koala Pad

A company called Chalk Board makes a bigger version of the Koala Pad called the PowerPad. Its drawing area is twelve inches square and the whole pad measures 20″ by 17″.

The advantage of this big drawing area is that you can get in more detail. But the large size also has a drawback—the PowerPad is too big to keep in your lap, and many people find it too clumsy to use comfortably.

Both Chalk Board and Koala publish a whole slew of learning programs and games to go with their products, and Chalk Board's are all neatly organized into subject areas and skill levels (but, annoyingly, they don't tell you what age range they're for).

Many of these programs come with **overlays**, transparent plastic sheets you put over the drawing area with markings on them that key into the software you're using.

One other type of input device is the **light pen**; with it, you actually draw right on the screen (that's what it looks like, anyway—what's really happening is more complicated than that).

Drawing on the screen sounds perfect, but there are two problems—

- it's hard to hold your hand up to the screen all the time (your shoulder gets tired, and that can make your hand shake)

- light pens are expensive, usually a couple of hundred dollars or more, while Koala Pads cost less than $100 most places and joysticks cost even less.

a light pen drawing directly on the screen

Well, having gone through all those input devices, let's see how an actual graphics program works. The one I've chosen is KoalaPainter, which comes with the Koala Pad. I'll give you a detailed description of KoalaPainter, so you'll not only get a sense of what a graphics program can do, but also how you actually go about using one.

KoalaPainter

Most software uses **menus** to tell you what you can do. Like the menus in restaurants, which tell you what foods you can order, the menus in computer programs tell you what commands you can order.

KoalaPainter's main menu is a nice full one. At the top are fifteen boxes; each has the name of a command and a little picture—called an **icon**—in it.

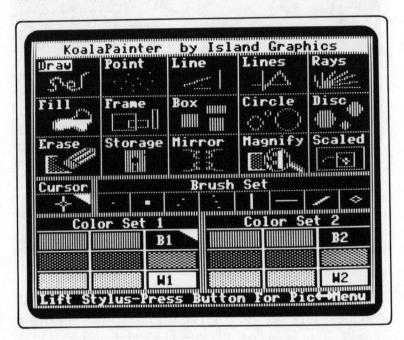

KoalaPainter's main menu

(By the way, if you're wondering who "Island Graphics" is, they're the people who actually wrote the program; Koala is the publisher.)

The box in the upper left corner is labelled "Draw" and that word is **highlighted** (or **reversed**)—that is, it's written as dark letters on a light background, instead of as light letters on a dark background like the names in the other menu boxes. (Highlighting works the other way too; if most of the screen is dark on light, the highlighted item will be light on dark.)

The fact that Draw is highlighted means it's **selected**—in other words, that's what you're going to get, unless you make another choice. To see what the Draw command produces, you have to leave the menu. The last line of the menu tells you how to do that. You lift the stylus off the Koala Pad (if you happen to be pressing it down) and push either of the buttons.

This gives you a blank screen to draw your pictures on (called the "picture screen"). When you touch the Koala Pad with the stylus, the cursor appears—a flickering cross with a circle in the middle of it.

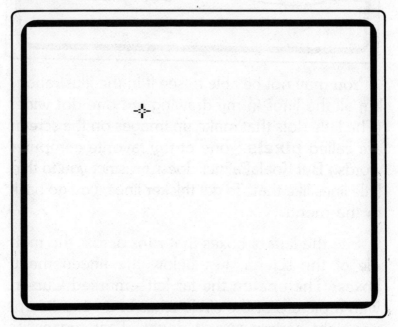

Now all you do is hit the right button on the Koala Pad and the cursor will make a line wherever you move it, until you hit the right button again. If your hand is as unsteady as mine is, you'll end up with something that looks like this:

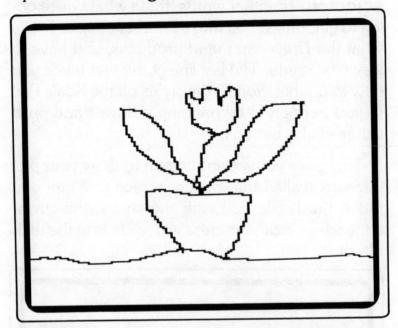

You may not be able to see it in the illustration, but all the lines in my drawing are one dot wide. (The little dots that make up images on the screen are called **pixels**—one of my favorite computer words.) But KoalaPainter doesn't restrict you to thin little lines like that. To get thicker lines, you go back to the menu.

See the line of boxes that runs across the middle of the screen, just below the fifteen menu boxes? The one on the far left—marked Cursor, with a picture of the circle cross in it—has its upper right corner turned down. That means it's selected, and that the lines in your drawings will all be one pixel wide. But you can select any of the eight boxes marked Brush Set, and when you go to the picture screen, you'll get what's in the box, instead of the regular cursor.

Let's select the box on the far right, the one with a diamond in it. When you draw with the diamond, you get lines that are five pixels wide:

The other brush shapes give you different kinds of cursors, and therefore different kinds of lines. For example, the box that has two dots in it gives you two parallel lines and the one with three, three.

The next command after Draw is Point; it lets you make individual dots rather than lines. You just touch the stylus down wherever you want the dot (or whatever brush shape you've selected); and when you hit either button, it gets deposited there.

The Draw command is great for freehand drawings, when you want the line to follow the cursor wherever it goes. But it's almost impossible to draw straight lines with it; that's what the Line, Lines and Rays commands are for.

With Line, you put the cursor where you want the line to start and then hit either button. As you move the cursor, the line stretches from that point, almost as if you were stretching a rubber band. As you move back toward the starting point, the line shortens; if you move all the way back, it disappears.

Because of the way Line works, it lets you adjust a line until it's straight. Let's say that, because your hand-eye coordination (like mine) isn't all that it could be, you start off with a jagged line like the one on the left in the illustration below. You just

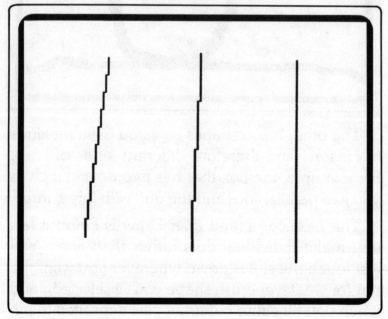

edge the cursor over until you get a line that looks like the middle one, and finally you get it just right (like the line on the right). At that point, you hit the button, and you've got a perfectly straight line.

The Lines command works the same way as Line, but it lets you draw any number of connected lines, as its icon illustrates. With Rays, you can make lines that fan out from one point. One thing it's good for is drawing sunbursts, like the one below:

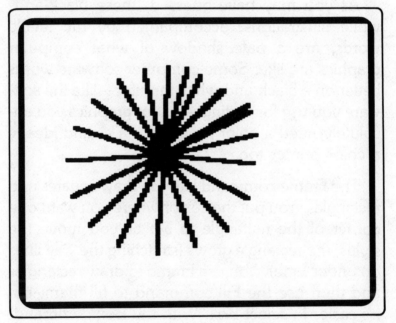

The Fill command lets you fill any enclosed shape with one of the colors at the bottom of the menu.

At all times in KoalaPainter, one of the colors at the bottom of the menu is selected. You haven't been able to see it, but all the lines I've been drawing so far have been in that selected color, whatever it happened to be at the time. (Don't worry about the fact that the colors are grouped into two "sets.")

Since you can't see the colors, I'll tell you that you get: a rich royal blue, a very nice gold, a terrific pink (my personal favorite—it's a pity you can't see it), a light kelly green, and a whole range of blue, green, red and gold check patterns that all look like ugly upholstery fabrics from the '50s.

As you may have guessed, these black-and-white illustrations, accompanied by my feeble words, are a pale shadow of what computer graphics are like. Some computer software works better on a black-and-white monitor—like the software you use for writing—but for graphics you absolutely need a color monitor or TV, and ideally a color printer too.

The Frame command lets you draw squares and rectangles. You put the cursor where you want one corner of the rectangle to be; as you move the stylus, the rectangle grows (stretching the way lines do under Line). You use Frame to draw rectangles and then use the Fill command to fill them, but it's easier to select Box. With the Box command, the rectangle fills in with the selected color the minute you're done drawing it.

Circle and Disc work the same way as Frame and Box. You start where you want the center of the circle to be and work out. Circle makes a hollow shape, and Disc makes one that's filled with color.

(What is it with this fancy misspelling of "disk?" You see it everywhere these days. It must be some kind of creeping brain disease.)

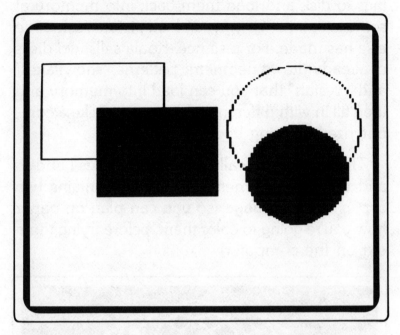

from left to right: a Frame, Box, Circle and Disc

With all these commands—Line, Lines, Rays, Frame, Box, Circle and Disc—different brush shapes give you different lines, just as they do with the Draw command.

You use Erase to wipe out a drawing and start over, and to choose what color you want for the background of the new drawing. Since it covers the entire screen with one color, Erase always gives me a hard decision to make: Should I color the whole screen that luscious pink and draw on it in green, or should I color the screen green and draw on it in pink?

The Storage command lets you save your drawings to disk and load them back into memory at some later time. Or you can load pictures someone else has made. For instance, Koala sells two disks of already-drawn geometric patterns, "snowflakes" and "crystals" that you can load into memory and then fill in with different colors—sort of like a computerized coloring book.

These disks are called Coloring Series I and II, and with each comes a book that contains two copies of each image (so you can plan on paper how you're going to color them, before trying them out on the computer).

image from KoalaWare Coloring Series II

The next command is my favorite. When you select Mirror, exact copies of everything you draw appear in all four corners of the screen. (You use Mirror in addition to another drawing command.) To create the four screens shown below, I selected Draw and the square brush. In the first screen, I've just put the cursor down and hit one of the buttons. As you can see, four cursors have appeared instead of one.

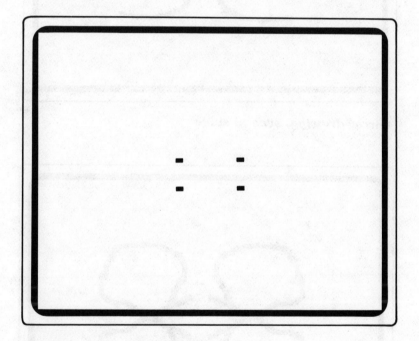

beginning of mirror drawing

The next three screens show the mirror drawing in progress—

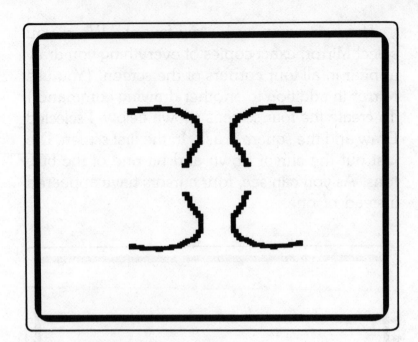

mirror drawing, second stage

mirror drawing, third stage

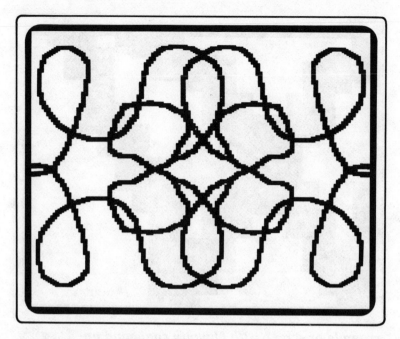

mirror drawing, finished

I love the Mirror command because it makes whatever you do look beautiful, even if you're a klutz like me. (I just wish you could see that last screen in color.)

The next command—Magnify—is wonderful too. It lets you zoom into the image on the screen so that each individual dot of color is maybe a quarter of an inch across. Since you use Magnify in addition to other commands, you can do all the drawings and shapes I've just described, but see them in incredible detail. You can even use Magnify with Mirror; the possibilities are mind-boggling.

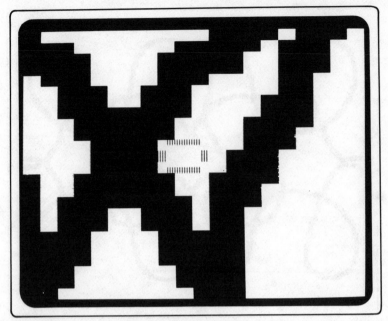

*example of screen with **Magnify** command on*

The last KoalaPainter command—Scaled—is a mystery to me. I can see how it works on the screen, but I haven't the faintest idea what you use it for, and the manual doesn't tell me.

Well, that was anticlimactic. But it doesn't matter: If that long description of KoalaPainter has turned you on to computer graphics, you don't need some sort of rah-rah finish; if it hasn't, a rah-rah finish wouldn't help.

Computer Colorworks publishes a program similar to KoalaPainter; it's called Flying Colors. Other graphics programs I've heard good things about are Paint (Reston Publishing), PictureWriter (Scarborough) and Doodle! (City Software).

On to music!

Chapter 4

Making Music on a Computer

My experiences with music have not been good. In grammar school, whenever I sang in a chorus, the teacher would always whisper to me, "Arthur, why don't you just mouth the words?"

In high school, I tried to learn to play the cornet, but I dropped the class when the teacher told me I had a tone "halfway between a kazoo and a New Year's horn."

So I figured that if a program could help someone like me actually write music, it would be a miracle. Well, the miracle happened. Using a music program called Songwriter (published by Scarborough), I composed several pieces of music (I guess you could call them that), and while I wouldn't go so far as to say that any of them are actually any good, I've listened to them many, many times and I'm still not tired of them. (I played them for a friend of mine who's a good jazz musician and he just couldn't stop laughing. But who cares?—*I* love them.)

I looked at more than fifty programs while doing the research for this book and Songwriter was far and away my personal favorite. I probably spent more time with it than with all the rest of the software put together, staying up late into the night composing my deranged little songs.

While Songwriter is loading itself into memory, it plays a little snatch of lovely music, a taste of things to come. Then it presents this screen:

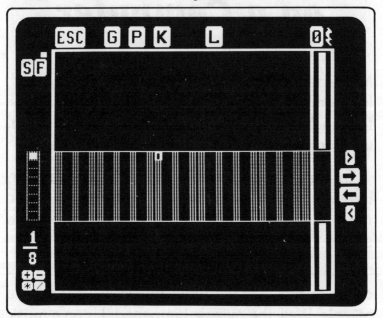

The bar across the middle looks like the keyboard of a piano, with the same pattern of white and black notes. It isn't a whole keyboard, of course, just 2½ octaves—thirty notes or so—but that's all you really need. If you look in the middle of the keyboard, you'll see that there's a little white square with a black center sitting on one of the notes. This is Songwriter's equivalent of a cursor.

Composing a song couldn't be simpler. You move the cursor around with the < , > and arrow keys. When you get to a note you want to record, you hit the spacebar. If you want to hear a note without recording it, you hit RETURN. To erase notes, you hit X.

When you hit the spacebar, the note appears above the keyboard. The next note you hit pushes that one up toward the top of the screen, as if you were writing them on a scroll. I've recorded a few notes to show you how it works:

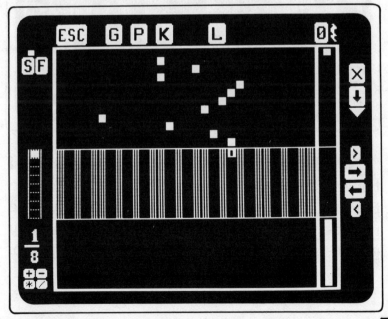

All the notes so far have been eighth notes; you can tell that by the ⅛ in the lower left corner, and also by how long they are. But Songwriter can do everything from whole notes to 48th notes.

In the screen below, you can see three eighth notes from before (the others have been pushed off the top). Then there's a quarter note and a half note. Finally I put in a bunch of 48th notes (I like them because they're so small and cute, and they make a great, burbling sound).

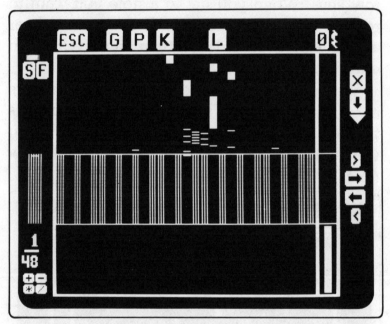

Now I've already written a song of sorts. All I have to do to play it is hit P. Songwriter goes to the start of the song and scrolls the notes you've recorded past the keyboard, playing them as they go by—sort of like a computerized player piano.

You can:
- stop the scroll at any time and begin again from that point
- walk through the song note by note, backwards or forwards
- delete old notes
- insert new ones. With all these capabilities, it's easy to edit the song.

You can also control the tempo of the song (how fast or slow it plays). In the upper left corner of the screen are the letters S and F with a small square above them. You can't see it, but that square is moving back and forth. To increase the tempo, you just hit F; the square starts moving faster, and the song is played faster. (Vice versa, of course, for S.) And with a different pair of commands, you can jump right to the fastest and the slowest tempo.

When you've got a song you like, you can save it on disk. Then you can edit it some more and save it under a different name. You can also load songs previously recorded into memory, either to work on them or just to listen to them.

The Songwriter disk comes with a whole library of wonderful music. You have a choice of over thirty pieces—three by Bach, five by Telemann, a couple of Irish ballads, the William Tell Overture, children's songs, and a lot more. It's interesting to study the pattern of notes while you listen to this music, and then go back and work on your own songs. Here's an interesting pattern from Telemann:

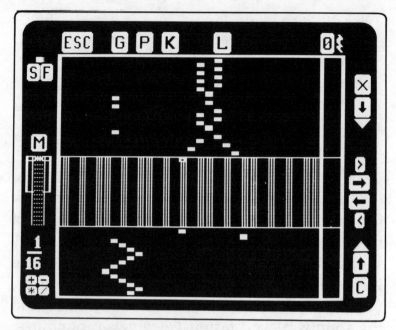

Georg Philipp Telemann (1681–1767) meets Songwriter

The connection between patterns on notes of the screen and patterns of notes in your ear is part of the theory behind Songwriter. The authors purposely decided not to show the music on the screen the way it's usually written, because they figured that would get in the way of your learning to make those connections. Songwriter doesn't even show you the letter names of the notes on the screen unless you specifically request them.

In addition to all its other capabilities, Songwriter lets you insert songs from the disk into songs that you're working on, save little snatches of musical ideas and stick them in the song wherever you want, and print out a list of the notes of your song (along with how long each note lasts). The program comes with a cable for connecting your computer to a stereo.

It also has an excellent reference card. A **reference card** is just what it sounds like—a piece of cardboard with all of a program's commands on it (or at least all of the important ones). You put it near your computer to refer to while running the program, so you don't have to look through the manual. Some programs don't need reference cards but, in general, they're a nice thing to have.

Another good music-writing program is Music Construction Set (Electronic Arts). Unlike Songwriter, it shows music the way it's usually written, with notes on a staff. The authors of Songwriter would say that this isn't as good for getting the patterns of music deep down into your brain, but even if that's true, Music Construction Set does teach you how to write and read sheet music, and that's a useful skill.

Now that you know about writing music, the next chapter will tell you how computers can help you write words.

Chapter 5

A GRIM SMILE FLICKERED, ACROSS OUR HERO'S FACE ...

Writing on a Computer

Word processing

Writing on a computer is called **word processing** and it's the main thing people actually use their computers for. When they buy them, they think they're going to mostly play games or program or something, but they end up doing more writing than anything else. So it's good to know that there are a lot of really excellent word processing programs that run on home computers.

I'll talk about one of them—Homeword from Sierra On-Line—in detail, to give you an idea of the kinds of things a good word processing program can do.

The package Homeword comes in is one of the most complete I've ever seen; it contains—in addition to the disk with the program on it—

- a cassette tape that teaches you how to use the program
- a transcript of the tape (the words on the tape written out on paper), in case you don't have a cassette player
- a manual
- a reference card
- four labels that say "Homeword document disk" (a **document** is any piece of writing, from a shopping list to a poem to a term paper)
- a little pamphlet on how to use and take care of disks. Ah, if only all software packages could be like this!

Like KoalaPainter, Homeword uses a lot of icons. There are six that run across the bottom of the main menu, and when you first enter it, the File icon—it looks like a filing cabinet—is selected (that's why it has a box around it).

With graphics programs, games and many other kinds of software, there are a wide variety of input

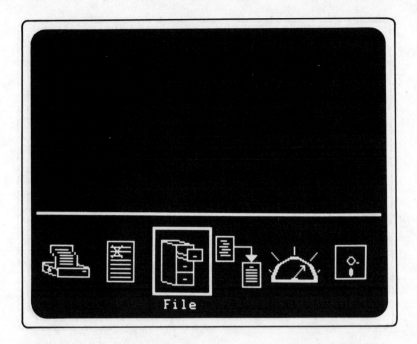

File

Homeword main menu

devices you can use—a joystick, a keyboard, a
Koala Pad, and so on. But for word processing,
you stick pretty much to the keyboard. For example, to move the box around to select other
Homeword icons, you use the arrow keys on your
keyboard. To choose the icon that's selected, you
hit the RETURN key.

But before we do either of those things, let's write
something. To get to the writing area, you use a
third key. It's marked ESC and is called the
ESCAPE key (because you use it to escape from
one place and go to another).

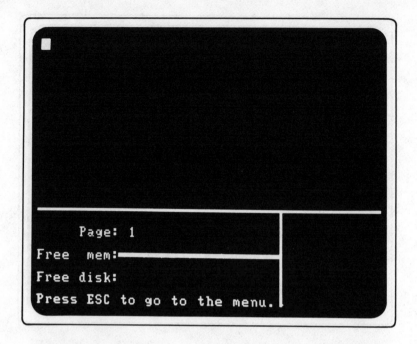

```
        Page: 1
Free   mem:
Free  disk:
Press ESC to go to the menu.
```

In the illustration above, the blank space at the top of the screen is where you write. At the bottom of the screen is some information about the document you're writing. The first piece of information is "Page 1," and it's obvious what that tells you.

The line after "Free mem" lets you know how much of the computer's memory you have left. As you can see, I have a lot left, because I haven't written anything yet. When the Free mem line gets short, it's time to save whatever you've written onto disk (actually, you should do this quite often, just to make sure you don't accidentally lose any of your work).

The line after "Free disk" tells you how crowded the disk is. Mine is pretty crowded, because I still have the disk with Homeword on it in the drive. When the Free disk line gets short, it's time to erase some old files you don't need anymore, or start a new disk.

The box in the lower right corner shows you what the page you're writing will look like when you "print it out" on paper. It's blank now, because we haven't written anything yet. Hold on a minute while I fix that:

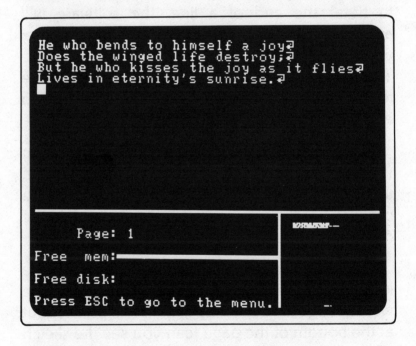

William Blake (1757–1827) meets Homeword (the poem is called Eternity)

If you're ever really hung up on someone, this poem is a sure-fire cure. Just lock yourself in a room and recite it a couple of million times.

I typed that poem just the way I would on an electric typewriter, hitting RETURN at the end of each line. (That funny little hooked arrow shows all the places where I hit RETURN.) But normally I wouldn't even have to do that, because Homeword, like most good word processing programs, has **word wrap**.

"Word wrap" means that if a word is too long to fit at the end of a line, the software will automatically stick it at the start of the next line; you just keep on typing and don't think about it. The only time you hit RETURN is when you come to the end of a paragraph, or when you want to end a line early (as in a poem, for example).

I made some mistakes when typing in the poem (I always do), and to correct them, I just backed up with the DELETE key, erasing as I went. (You can also use the arrow keys to move around in the document.)

Now that I've typed something, the box in the lower right corner shows a sketch of the page. The words "Page 1" will be automatically printed out at the bottom of the page (can you see the sketch of them down there?).

Word wrap and automatic page numbering are just two of the many things that make word processing a lot easier than using a typewriter. Let's go back to the main menu so I can tell you about some of the others.

The icon just to the left of File is Edit (it looks like a sheet of writing with a big X on it). When you choose Edit, you get a whole new menu (shown in the illustration below).

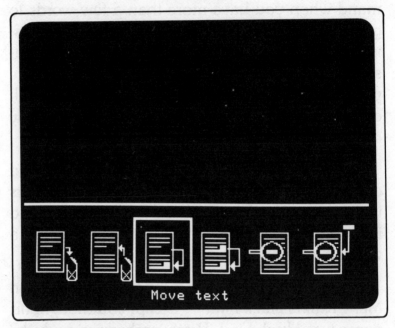

Move text

Homeword edit menu

The icon that comes up selected when you enter the Edit menu is for Move Text. This command lets you grab a bunch of words, pull them out of where they are in the document, and stick them in somewhere else. Move Text is great for reorganizing something you've written. To write this book, for example, I must have moved more blocks of text than the number of hairs on your head (well, more than the number on my head, anyway).

Another command is Copy Text. This works the same way as Move Text, but when the block of text goes to the new place, it stays in the old place as well.

You can also Erase Text—take a bunch of text and throw it in the trash can. You use this command when you have more than a few words to get rid of and don't want to spend the time erasing them with the DELETE key. And you can Insert Erased Text. This command lets you change your mind, take the erased text out of the trash can and put it back in the document. (You can only do it with the last piece of text you erased.)

Impressed? You ain't seen nothin' yet. The Find command lets you find every place a word occurs in the document. The Find and Replace command is even more amazing; it not only lets you find a word, it lets you change it to anything you want.

So let's say you wrote a long book report on Mark Twain's *Huck Finn* — except you thought his name was Hunk Fink. Pretty embarrassing, huh? (also pretty unlikely). Anyway—instead of having to retype the whole paper, you could just go through and change every occurrence of Hunk Fink to Huck Finn. It would take just a few seconds, and you'd have a completely corrected paper to print out.

(With word processing, you do all your writing on the screen, and only print out on paper at the end. Even if you've already printed something out, you can just make your changes and print it out again. After all, the computer is doing the work, not you; you can go read a book while it's happening.)

That's it for the Edit menu. Let's go back to the main menu and see what else Homeword can do. (I'll give you another picture of the main menu so you don't have to keep flipping pages back to the last one.)

Homeword main menu (again)

The File icon gives you a menu where you can save a document to disk, get a document you saved on the disk earlier and put it into memory (by itself or into the middle of another document), and chain documents together.

The icon to the right of File shows a messy looking page turning into a neat one. This is for the Layout menu, which lets you decide things like how wide the margins will be when your document prints out, whether it will be single-, double- or triple-spaced, and how far you want the paragraphs indented. You can even make parts of your text **boldfaced**, and have lines of text automatically print out at the top and bottom of each page (called **headers** and **footers**).

The next icon over looks like the dial that tells you what floor an elevator is at—one of those old-fashioned elevators you find in some department stores and office buildings. This is for the Customize menu and it lets you...well...customize Homeword to your own taste. For example, you can ask Homeword to always automatically save the last two versions of your document, instead of just the last one.

The icon on the far right, which looks like a disk, gives you the Disk utilities menu. This lets you prepare a disk (so that you can save your documents onto it), erase a document from the disk, or find out what documents are already on a disk.

Finally, we come to the icon on the far left. It looks like a printer and—not surprisingly—that's where you go when you're ready to put your document on paper. (The Print menu also lets you see how your finished document will look on the screen, before you print it out.)

Isn't word processing amazing? Hopefully this description of Homeword has helped you see how much easier and how much more fun it is to write something when you're word processing instead of typing.

Other word processing programs I've heard good things about are:
- PFS:Write (Software Publishing Co.)
- the AppleWorks Word Processor (Apple)
- Bank Street Writer (Broderbund)
- the Milliken Word Processor (Milliken)

Hayden Software also puts out two good word processing programs. One is designed to be used at home and is called The Writer; it's more powerful but also harder to use than Homeword. One of the nicest things about it, though, is that if you ever need a really versatile word processing program like the ones they use in businesses, you can move up to PIE Writer. All the documents you created with The Writer will work with PIE Writer, and so will all the commands you learned (you'll just have to learn some additional ones, to take advantage of PIE Writer's special abilities).

Checking your spelling

No matter how powerful a word processing program is, there's one thing it can't do—correct your spelling. For that, you need another kind of program, called a **spelling checker**.

When I first heard about spelling checkers, I couldn't figure out how they worked. After all, how can a dumb computer tell when you've spelled a word rong? Actually, it's very simple. All spelling checkers contain dictionaries of correctly spelled words. When they check something you've written, they simply take each word of it and see if they can find it in their dictionary (this is something computers can do very fast).

If the word isn't on their list, they say, "Hey, this word isn't in my dictionary," and then they let you decide if that's because you misspelled it, or because it's the name of your Uncle Dorkley in Kokomo and "dorkley" naturally wouldn't be in their dictionary.

One spelling checker that's fast and easy-to-use is called The Speller; it's published by Hayden Software as a companion to The Writer, although you can use it with a number of other word processing programs as well. Two other spelling checkers I hear good things about are Bank Street Speller (Broderbund) and PFS:Proof (Software Publishing Company).

I'll just describe The Speller briefly, because the fun of spelling checkers isn't using them—it's the result they produce.

When you enter the program, it asks you for the name of the file (document) you want to check. I used Homeword to make up one called ROTE RONG. As soon as The Speller begins checking a file, it tells you how many words are in it. While it's looking through its main dictionary for words that match, it gives you a running count of how far it's gotten (at the bottom left on the screen).

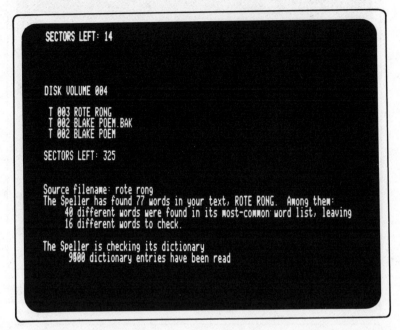

```
SECTORS LEFT: 14



DISK VOLUME 004

  T 003 ROTE RONG
  T 002 BLAKE POEM.BAK
  T 002 BLAKE POEM

SECTORS LEFT: 325


Source filename: rote rong
The Speller has found 77 words in your text, ROTE RONG.  Among them:
    40 different words were found in its most-common word list, leaving
    16 different words to check.

The Speller is checking its dictionary
    9500 dictionary entries have been read
```

When it finishes, it tells you how many words it couldn't find (and that therefore *might* be misspelled). Then it looks to see if you've created a dictionary of your own, with words that you use a lot but that aren't likely to be in a regular dictionary. For example, if you're in the Mafia, many of your documents will contain words like *consigliere* and *capo*. You don't want the spelling checker to always be asking you if those words are spelling mistakes, so you list them in your personal dictionary.

When The Speller has finished checking your dictionary (if you have one), it gives you the following information:

```
DISK VOLUME 004

  T 003 ROTE RONG
  T 002 BLAKE POEM.BAK
  T 002 BLAKE POEM

SECTORS LEFT: 325


Source filename: rote rong
The Speller has found 77 words in your text, ROTE RONG.  Among them:
    40 different words were found in its most-common word list, leaving
    16 different words to check.

The Speller is checking its dictionary
    20575 dictionary entries have been read
5 words were not in the dictionary and may be misspelled

The Speller is checking your dictionary, MYWORDS.WDS
    0 dictionary entries have been read
5 words were not in the dictionary and may be misspelled


Press RETURN to continue ■
```

The next screen gives you seven choices of what to do next:

```
The Speller has found 77 words in your text, ROTE RONG.  Among them:
    40 different words were found in its most-common word list, leaving
    16 different words to check.

5 words were not in the dictionary and may be misspelled




You may now:
    Display(D), Print(P), Check(C), Scan(S), Use(U), Review(R), or Exit(E)? ■

DISPLAY --- a list of suspect or valid words.
PRINT   --- a list of suspect or valid words.
CHECK   --- all suspect words one by one.
SCAN    --- your text, stopping to check all suspect words.
USE     --- an additional dictionary to check your words.
REVIEW  --- your previous word choices.
EXIT    --- save files and exit program.
```

Rather than run through them all, I'll go right to the one you're most likely to use—SCAN. This walks you through your file, stopping at each misspelled word. It points to the word and asks you to decide if it's spelled correctly or not. If it isn't, you can type in the correct spelling and The Speller will correct the file for you. If it is spelled correctly, you can add it to your dictionary so The Speller won't keep showing it to you. You can also decide to postpone your decision till later.

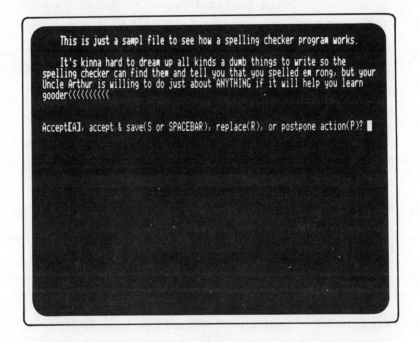

```
     This is just a sampl file to see how a spelling checker program works.

     It's kinna hard to dream up all kinds a dumb things to write so the
spelling checker can find them and tell you that you spelled em rong, but your
Uncle Arthur is willing to do just about ANYTHING if it will help you learn
gooder<<<<<<<<<<                            .


Accept[A], accept & save(S or SPACEBAR), replace(R), or postpone action(P)? ■
```

In the screen above, The Speller has walked through my file and stopped at each misspelled word. Now it's pointing to the fifth one —"gooder" (I could have sworn that was spelled right). Can you find the other four?

Time's up. The misspelled words are: sampl, kina, em and rong...hey, wait a minute—what's rong with rong?

Story telling

There's a wonderful series of books that go by the name of Choose Your Own Adventure™. As you read them, they keep asking you what you want to do. For example, if you meet an old wizard in a forest and he invites you to his hut for a cup of newt's eye soup, you can decide either to go with him or to continue on your way. At that point, the book "branches." If you go with him, you turn to page 27 (or whatever). If you don't, you turn to some other page.

Each branch branches again, and again, and again, so that the book may have 40 or 50 different endings, depending on the choices you've made. Instead of being organized in a straight line from beginning to end, the way most books are, the Choose Your Own Adventure books are organized more like a tree, with one root (the beginning) and lots of branches.

Story Tree (from Scholastic) is a program that lets you write branching stories on a computer. To get you warmed up, it offers three sample stories to read; you can even play with them and change them. Next, if you want, it will walk you through the creation of a detective story. Then you're on your own.

You write your story one screenful at a time

(since that's how people will read it). At the end of each screen, you have three choices:

- You can send the reader on to another screen automatically, without any choice. Usually you do this because you can't fit all the words you want onto just one screen.

- You can let the reader choose between two or more alternatives. For example, the last line of the screen might read:
  "Do you:
  a) open the door?
  b) hide in the closet?
  c) climb back up the chimney?"

Each choice sends the reader to a different screen.

- You can have the next screen decided by chance. For example, you can have the reader thrown into a snake pit 50% of the time, rescued by a flying saucer 30% of the time, and turned into a toadstool 20% of the time. The reader has no choice about it, and neither do you after you've decided on the percentages; the computer picks a screen each time by chance (so that if you went through that part of the story a hundred times, you'd get pretty close to 50 snake pits, 30 flying saucers and 20 toadstools, but if you went through it just twice, you might get two toadstools in a row).

Learning to type

Some things are just boring and there's no way around them. Learning to type is one of those things. It's a *really* useful thing to know how to do; in fact, it's probably the most useful thing I learned in high school (that's not saying much). But it is *bor-ing* to learn.

Ah, but computers change all that. In Master-Type (from Scarborough), you are a space station being attacked from all four corners of the screen by spaceships. Words appear in each of the corners and you have to type them correctly to destroy the ships coming in from the corners. If you don't type the word fast enough, or if you type it wrong and don't get it fixed in time, the spaceship crashes into you and destroys part of your shield. If this happens often enough, the screen goes crazy, the computer makes a lot of noise, and a message comes on that says, "The words win!"

MasterType sounds hard, and it is, but it starts off easy, with just one letter in each corner. You can control how fast the spaceships come at you, and how difficult the words are. It's really a lot of fun, although I'd hate to tell you how often the words win when I'm playing.

Well, that's a good sampling of some of the ways you can use computers for writing. Now for the chapter you've been waiting for—G*A*M*E*S!!!

Chapter   **6**

Playing Games (and Learning Things) on a Computer

You may have noticed that some of the programs I've talked about in earlier chapters look suspiciously like games, even though that's not what they're called. Actually, it's hard to draw the line between games and other kinds of learning programs.

In spite of that, a lot of adults seem to think that all games are a waste of time, no matter how complicated and interesting they are, and all learning programs are worthwhile, no matter how simple-minded and boring they are. In other words, unless something feels bad, it can't be any good for you.

This is nuts. Learning is fun. The more fun it is, the more you learn—and the more you learn, the more fun it is. It doesn't matter if a program is called a game or not; what matters is whether it's any good or not.

Now help me down off this soapbox, will you? Thanks.

In this chapter, I'll discuss four basic kinds of games: role-playing, strategy and logic, adventure, and word games.

Role-playing games

There used to be a magazine called Softalk and every year, it asked its readers what their favorite program was. Just about every year, the readers answered, "Wizardry!" Wizardry (by Sir-Tech) is a classic game of the type called "fantasy role-playing." It's been around for a while (winning the Softalk poll since 1978), so the authors have really got all the details worked out.

The first thing you do in a role-playing game is create a character. Wizardry gives you a choice of being a fighter, a mage (sort of like a witch), a priest, a thief, a bishop, a samurai, a lord or a ninja (a kind of fanatic Japanese warrior).

There are six basic characteristics—strength, intelligence, piety (which, in Wizardry, means the ability to cast spells), vitality (liveliness), agility (the

ability to move quickly and gracefully) and luck—
and each character has varying amounts of them.
A mage, for example, must have at least 11 points
worth of intelligence, a thief needs a minimum agility of 11, and so on.

Once you've figured out what kind of character
you want to be, you then have to decide:

- what "alignment" you are (good, evil or
  neutral)
- what race you are (human, elf, dwarf,
  gnome or hobbit)
- how much gold you have
- what equipment you have (everything
  from weapons to armor to magical things)
- etc. etc.

(Obviously, there are limits to how many good
things you can choose for yourself.)

As you can see, you could easily spend more
time just getting ready to play Wizardry than it takes
to play most other games all the way through.

Games of strategy and logic

This is the biggest category of games by far, and
I could even have included the next category—
adventure games—in it. Almost all games require
strategy and logic of one kind or another. Here are
a few of the best strategy games I know about:

Snooper Troops (Spinnaker) is a series of detective cases that you solve by collecting clues. You
drive around in your SnoopMobile, interview
suspects, take notes, take pictures, and try not to

get bumped off before you figure out who committed the crime. Case #1 is called The Granite Point Ghost, and Case #2 is called The Disappearing Dolphin (they're sold separately).

In Search of the Most Amazing Thing (Spinnaker) is an even more elaborate game. Your uncle, Smoke Bailey, found the Most Amazing Thing in the Whole Wide Galaxy when he was a boy, but then he lost it again. A very well-written and funny book comes with the program; called The Adventures of Smoke Bailey, it tells the story of how that happened.

Smoke is an old man now and he wants you to continue the search for the Most Amazing Thing. You can use his "B-liner"—a combination hot air balloon and dune buggy, and there's also a jetpack for travelling short distances. Smoke gives you valuable objects he's collected on his travels; you take them to the auction, sell them to the robots there, and use the chips you get to buy supplies for the B-liner.

Once the B-liner is all ready, you fly out over the Darksome Mire. The people you meet on the Mire belong to 25 different cultures, each with its own customs. Somewhere out there is the Most Amazing Thing, and the Mire People can help you find it. To get clues, you trade them songs you make up and chips you earned at the auction.

(You can see that this is not a game you can finish in one afternoon. It's like a good long book you hope will never end.)

When I was doing the research for this book, I went around asking people who know a lot about kids and computers what software they thought I should cover. Every one of them mentioned Rocky's Boots (from The Learning Company), and almost every one of them mentioned it first. I can see why—this is a program that really has everything.

One of the things I like best about Rocky's Boots is that you don't need to look at the manual at all. A lot of programs make that claim, but it's really true about Rocky's Boots. I'll prove it to you. The program begins with the screen you see below:

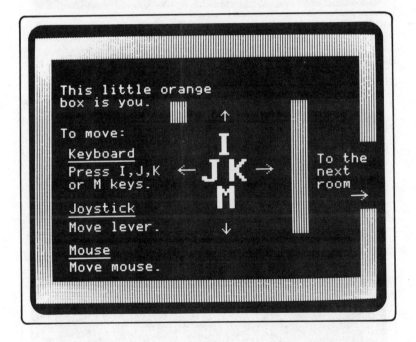

There's no way you could misunderstand that, is there? You move through the door on the right, and find yourself here:

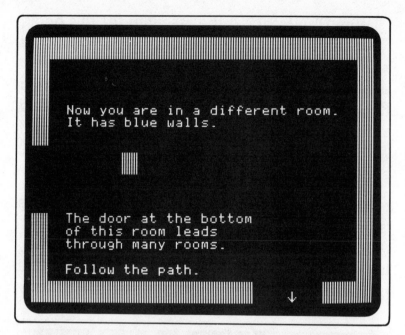

Now you are in a different room.
It has blue walls.

The door at the bottom
of this room leads
through many rooms.

Follow the path.

This is so simple that even a television newscaster could follow it. In the next room, you learn how to pick things up:

To pick up this bird,
run into it and
press the SPACEBAR,
the joystick BUTTON,
or the mouse BUTTON.

Put the bird down by
pressing SPACEBAR or
BUTTON again.

Now this may seem like a pretty simple-minded piece of software so far, but I'm only trying to show you how slowly it starts off, and how it just about makes it impossible for you to make a mistake.

But Rocky's Boots goes on to teach you—just as clearly and gradually as these first three screens—how to wire the kind of electronic circuits that make up computers. By the end of the game, you're building circuits of your own and playing games with them. Here's a simple example of one:

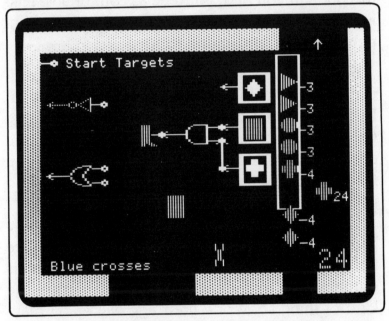

This is a machine for kicking blue crosses. Objects of different sizes and shapes glide by in that long vertical box. To the left of the box are three "sensors." The one on the bottom senses whether anything that goes by is a cross. The one above it senses whether anything that goes by is blue. The top sensor senses diamonds (so we don't need to hook that one up).

The two bottom sensors are connected by something called an "AND gate." That means that *both* the sensors have to be on for the current to flow through to the boot (so that it can kick the object that's going by).

If you're feeling a little lost, that's just because you haven't played your way through the game to this point. If you had, you'd be as comfortable talking about "sensors" and "AND gates" as about peanut butter and blue jeans.

Rocky's Boots lets you make *much* more complicated circuits than the one I just showed you. But to go really crazy, what you want is Robot Odyssey (another Learning Company game described in Chapter 8). In Robot Odyssey, you take the same skills you learn in Rocky's Boots and use them to build robots.

There are a number of good logic and strategy games published by Sunburst, but mostly they're for younger kids. The Factory is the most famous of them, and it's a good introductory game—the kind of thing someone your age will enjoy playing for a week or two and then get tired of, because you've learned all that it has to teach you. Some of the other Sunburst strategy games are The Incredible Laboratory, Code Quest, Fun House Maze and The King's Rule.

Adventure games

In a typical **adventure game**, you're trying to find some buried treasure, or rescue a damsel in distress, or save the galaxy, while avoiding werewolves, vampires and other villains that are trying to kill you. Only words, not pictures, appear on the screen, and you have to draw a map on a sheet of paper to find your way around. As you travel, you come across objects. When you do, it's a good idea to pick them up and carry them with you; you never know when you might need them.

The beginning of Zork III (from Infocom) gives you a good feeling for what adventure games are like. The screen reads:

"As in a dream, you see yourself tumbling down a great, dark staircase. All about you are shadowy images of struggles against fierce opponents and diabolical traps." Then you see a man with "long, silver hair dancing about him in a fresh breeze." He turns slowly toward you and says, "You have reached the final test, my friend. You are proved clever and powerful, but this is not yet enough. Seek me when you feel yourself worthy!"

On the next screen, "you are at the bottom of a seemingly endless stair, winding its way upward beyond your vision...To the south is a dark and winding trail. Your old friend, the brass lantern, is at your feet."

It seems pretty obvious that the lantern might come in handy at some point. So you type in: "Take lantern." Zork answers: "Taken." Next you might type: "Climb stairs." But Zork tells you that "the stairs are endless." So you say, "Go south." This command is acceptable to Zork, so off you go.

Next Zork tells you: "It is pitch black. You are likely to be eaten by a grue." If you're smart, you ask, "What is a grue?" Zork explains: "A grue is a sinister, lurking presence in the dark places of the earth. Its favorite diet is adventurers, but its insatiable appetite is tempered by its fear of light..."

I could go on (Zork certainly does), but that should give you a taste of it.

Normally you have to play an adventure game many, many times to get through it to the final goal. Each time you learn more about how to survive. For example, I got eaten by a grue twice before I realized I had to light the lamp I was carrying to keep them away (I'm not too bright).

The reason I say adventure games are really just a sub-category of strategy and logic games is that you have to think and plan to get through them. You need to draw a map, remember things like how to keep grues at bay, make decisions based on what you've learned, and so on. In other words, like everything that's fun, you learn from it.

Word games

As I said earlier (and will probably say again) I think memorization drills are a waste of time for anyone with more intelligence that a head of lettuce. But spelling is one area where memorization is unavoidable. That's because the way English words are spelled makes no sense.

Most other languages have logical rules for spelling; in other words, you can pretty much tell how a word is spelled from how it sounds. When people who grew up speaking a foreign language try to learn English spelling, they're flabbergasted by how disorganized and nonsensical it is.

Anyway, if you're going to have to memorize how words are spelled, you may as well have fun doing it. Spellicopter (from DesignWare) is a game that makes spelling drills about as much fun as they can be.

Spellicopter gives you a choice of 40 lists of 10

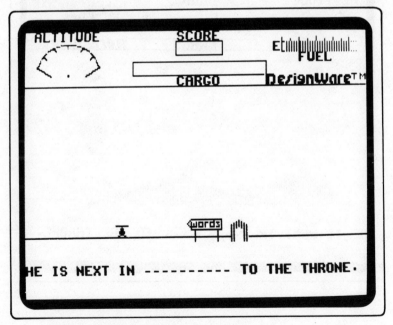

beginning Spellicopter screen

words each, at basic, intermediate or advanced levels of difficulty. You can also supply your own lists of words. When you've picked a list, Spellicopter shows it to you (if you want) and then puts you in a helicopter on a landing field. A sentence, with a blank space where the word you need to spell should be, is at the bottom of the screen. A little sign on the ground points the way to the "words."

You fly the helicopter with the joystick or with the I, J, K and M keys on your keyboard. On your way to the spelling area, you pass a screen full of clouds, hang gliders, balloons and blimps; if you bump into one of them, you crash.

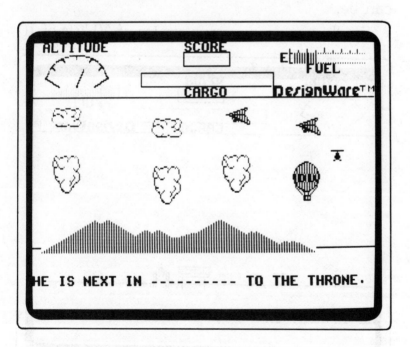

Then you get to a screen where the letters of the word you're trying to spell are scattered on the ground. You have to fly directly over the letters and pick them up in the right order to spell the word. At the more advanced skill levels, you have to avoid flying saucers at the same time. The flying saucers don't just glide by, they chase you—so you really have to pay some attention to keeping out of their way. Once you've spelled the word, you have to fly back to the first screen and land, still avoiding the flying saucers, clouds, aircraft, etc.

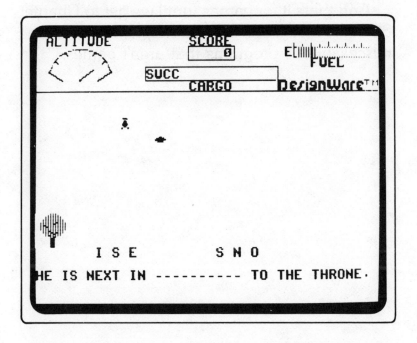

If you run out of fuel while doing all this, you crash and have to start over again. You lose points for that, as well as for crashing into anything. But you get bonus points for how much fuel you have left when you land.

As you can see, Spellicopter is a whole lot more fun that sitting down with a list of words and memorizing them.

DesignWare also makes another spelling game, Crypto Cube. Crossword Magic (L & S Computerware) is another kind of word game that's worth mentioning. It lets you make up crossword puzzles and challenge your friends with them.

And that's it for games (until we get to Chapter 8). In the meantime, the next chapter looks at some miscellaneous programs that aren't games.

Chapter 7

Other Things You Can Do on a Computer

Making posters (and a lot more)

I've seen plenty of hard-to-use software in my time—so confusing and frustrating it could make a statue cry. I've also seen my share of software that's easy-to-use (the Apple IIc "system utilities"—a bunch of little programs that do specific jobs like copy disks—are one example).

But I think that The Print Shop (from Broder-bund) must be the *easiest-to-use* program of them all. It's another one of those programs that doesn't even begin to need a manual. Here's what the main menu looks like:

This first menu gives you the choice of making a greeting card, a sign, some personalized letterhead to write your letters on, or a banner. (You can also do some other things that I'll come back to later.) Banners are a lot of fun, so let's choose that one.

As you can see, the picture in the little box on the right changes with what's selected. The banner you can make isn't quite as big as the one that plane is pulling, but it is huge.

Next The Print Shop asks you which typeface you want the banner to be written in, and shows you a sample of each one in the box at the bottom of the screen. (You can also see complete alphabets of all the typefaces on the handy reference card Broderbund provides.) It's a nice range of choices.

Next you get a choice of solid or outline type, and then you type out what you want the message to be. Then comes this screen:

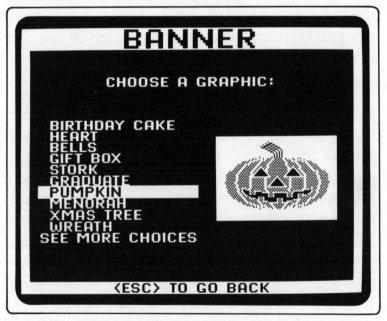

The Print Shop gives you an incredible selection of images to use in your banner (or your greeting card, sign or letterhead)—sixty in all! What's more, they're all very nicely drawn (you get to see them in the little box on the right, and also on the reference card, where they're also identified by number so you can just ask for one directly).

You get a choice of a birthday cake, heart, bells, gift box, stork, graduate (with diploma and mortarboard), pumpkin, menorah, Christmas tree, wreath, rose, cupid, Apple logo, ice cream cone, cup and saucer, champagne bottle and glass, candlestick, light bulb, sun shining over a cloud, outer space scene, piano, drum, trumpet, musical notes, top hat, skull and crossbones, sailboat, antique car, train, rocket, house, bag full of money, computer, floppy disk, scales, robot, alarm clock, big question mark, yin-yang symbol, quill and scroll, dog, cat, teddy bear, turtle, pig, rabbit, penguin, dove, butterfly, roast turkey and ten different patterns! I think you just might be able to find something to use in there.

After you pick a picture, The Print Shop asks you if you're ready to print out, and the next thing you know, you're holding in your hands an enormous customized banner, 8½ inches tall and several feet long.

Now there wasn't a step in that whole process where you had any doubt at all about what to do. And the results look great, whether it's a banner, a sign, a greeting card or letterhead. The program even comes with some beautiful orange-gold computer paper to do your printouts on, and with envelopes the same color to put your greeting cards in.

If this were all The Print Shop did, it would be worth buying not merely the program but a printer too, just so you could take advantage of it. But that's *not* all the Print Shop does. There's a menu item called Screen Magic (that little picture of the sorcerer looks great in color, by the way) which gives two separate sets of spectacularly beautiful kaleidoscopic images on the screen.

They just go on and on and on, each image more breathtaking than the last. (There's no point in trying to show you one here; they really depend on the colors.) If you see a pattern that particularly knocks you out, you can "freeze" it, save it to disk, and call it back whenever you like. You can also put text over any of these frozen screens, and print them out (with or without text).

Well, you get the idea—The Print Shop is really a great program.

Connecting with bulletin boards

Another interesting thing you can do with a computer is use it to call other computers. To do that, you need something called a **modem** (MOE-dum), which is a device that connects your computer to the telephone lines and turns the signals your computer puts out into sound. (It also works the other way—taking sounds from another computer off the phone line and turning them into signals your computer can understand.)

The computer you're calling has to have an **auto-answer modem** (one that automatically answers the phone and connects the computer to it), unless someone is there to answer the phone and hook up the computer personally.

There are three main kinds of computers you might want to talk to. First, there are **informa-**

tion networks like CompuServe and The Source. These are huge computers that contain a lot of different **data bases** (collections of information on just about any subject you can imagine). They cost money to join and also charge you for each minute you spend talking to their computer.

Then there are **bulletin boards**—computers you can call up, leave messages on, and read the messages other people have left. Usually bulletin boards are set up by a small organization or an individual, although the information networks have bulletin boards too. Bulletin boards are free, and usually operate 24 hours a day.

Finally, you can use your computer to send a message directly to a friend's computer. This is a little like writing a letter and is called **electronic mail**. Why, you may ask, should you type out a message to someone who you can just call up on the phone and talk to directly? Well, for one thing, you can leave the message at any time; your friend doesn't have to be home. And also, if you hook your computer into a **network** of other computers, you can have three-way (or ten-way) conversations—a little like being on CB radio.

There's another way to send electronic mail. The information networks let you have **mailboxes**—places where letters to you can be stored. You just get on the network, open your mailbox, and read your mail.

There's even a network whose main purpose is

sending electronic mail—MCI Mail. It gives you a mailbox for free, and doesn't charge you for time on the network, just for each letter you send—and even those are cheap (all of this could change, of course, but that's how it is now).

I could write a whole book about computer networking, but hopefully that gives you a little taste of some of the possibilities.

Business software

If you weren't a kid, you'd feel a lot of pressure to use your computer to help you make more money, instead of just to have fun. But even if you don't feel pressured to use business software, some of it does neat things.

For example, PFS:Graph (Software Publishing) will take numbers you put into it and make a line graph, a bar graph or a pie graph out of them. You can even change from one type of chart to another. Charts and graphs can really jazz up the papers you do for school.

Record-keeping software can also help with schoolwork. And you can use it to keep track of anything you collect—baseball cards, stamps, comic books, or whatever. It's good for mailing lists too. I hear good things about three record-keeping programs: the AppleWorks Data Base (Apple), PFS:File (Software Publishing) and Phi Beta Filer (Scarborough).

Some companies put together business software

packages, made up of a number of different programs that do different jobs but that all work together and share information (this is called **integrated** software). People rave about AppleWorks, which contains a word processing program, a "data base manager" (record-keeping program) and a "spreadsheet" (a program for predicting how much money you'll have in the future if you do different things today).

And Software Publishing Corp. makes a series of integrated programs that includes PFS:Write (word processing), PFS:Proof (spelling checker), PFS:Graph (chart-making), PFS:File (record-keeping), PFS:Access (communicating over phone lines) and several others.

Even if you don't have any use for all this business software yourself, be glad it's around; it can help you convince your parents that they—not just you—would benefit if the family had a decent computer.

Now for the *really* incredible stuff.

Chapter 8

Really Incredible Things You Can Do on a Computer

By now you realize that there are a lot of things computers can do really well. But the thing they do best of all is called **simulation**. In a simulation, the computer imitates something that happens in real life. For example, before NASA sends a rocket into space, they run computer simulations of the flight to find out what would happen if something on the rocket broke.

Some of the programs I talked about in earlier

chapters are technically simulations. You could look at Songwriter as a simulation of a player piano, or at Rocky's Boots as a simulation of electronic circuits. But in this chapter I discuss the really far-out simulations, the ones that will knock your socks off (not necessarily when I describe them, but when you play them).

Pinball Construction Set

Whenever people talk about simulations, the first one they usually mention is Pinball Construction Set (published by Electronic Arts). And no wonder. This incredible program actually lets you build your own custom pinball machines on the screen. When the program comes up, the screen looks like this:

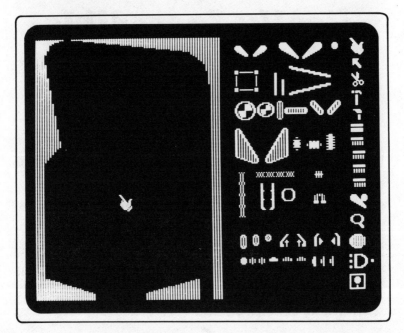

On the left is the area where you build the machine. On the right is the "parts box." Basically all you do is grab things in the parts box and paste them wherever you want them. When you're done, you just start playing.

Some of the parts you have to choose from are:

- Flippers — You use these to keep the ball in play, just as you do on a regular pinball machine. You always want one pair at the bottom, so you can try to stop the ball from rolling out, but you can put them anywhere else you want too.

- Bumpers — Round shapes that kick the ball away (kicks are forceful).

- Polygons — These can be just about any shape. They bounce the ball away (a bounce is more gentle than a kick).

- Slingshots — Triangles that kick the ball away on one long side and bounce it away from the other two sides.

- Kickers — Rectangles that kick on the ends and bounce on the sides.

- Ball hoppers — These catch and hold two balls, but when you get a third in, all three are released at the same time.

- Ball eaters — When a ball hits one of these, it disappears from the face of the earth.

Also in the parts box are scissors, a hammer and an arrow (for changing the shapes of polygons), a paintbrush (for changing the color of things), and a magnifier (for really detailed customizing).

It may sound like there are no limits to what Pinball Construction Set can do, but that's not true; you can't build a pinball machine with more than 128 parts!

There's no way to demonstrate how great this program is on the pages of a book, of course. But to give you an idea of the kind of things you can build, the next illustration shows you one of the five demo pinball machines that come on the disk. Just playing them is worth the price of the software.

Microbe

If you've ever seen the movie *Fantastic Voyage*, where Raquel Welch and a bunch of guys get shrunk down and sent travelling through somebody's bloodstream, you have the basic idea of how this next simulation works. But the movie was really dumb and unrealistic, and this game is really intelligent and very realistic. It's called Microbe (Synergistic Software) and one of its two authors is an actual doctor.

When the game starts, you're presented with a series of cases like the one below. (If you want the game to last more than a few minutes, you have to start taking notes now.) Because a doctor helped write this program, all the medical terms used are

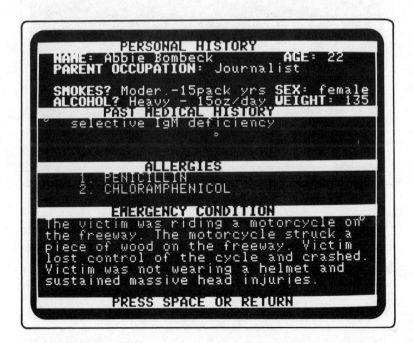

```
              PERSONAL HISTORY
NAME: Abbie Bombeck              AGE: 22
PARENT OCCUPATION: Journalist

SMOKES? Moder.-15pack yrs SEX:  female
ALCOHOL? Heavy - 15oz/day WEIGHT: 135
           PAST MEDICAL HISTORY
    selective IgM deficiency


              ALLERGIES
       1. PENICILLIN
       2. CHLORAMPHENICOL
           EMERGENCY CONDITION
The victim was riding a motorcycle on
the freeway. The motorcycle struck a
piece of wood on the freeway. Victim
lost control of the cycle and crashed.
Victim was not wearing a helmet and
sustained massive head injuries.

       PRESS SPACE OR RETURN
```

accurate. In fact, Microbe is even used to train medical students!

When you choose a case you think you'd like to cure, you get a screen that's full of even more medical language. Fortunately, the program provides you with a "physician's reference manual" that lists all the terms you need to know. If you play Microbe enough, you begin to know the terms and what they stand for without having to look at the manual. (That's the point, of course.)

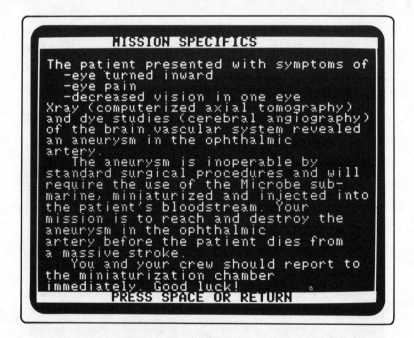

Once you've taken notes on this second screen, you and your crew and the submarine you'll be travelling in are put into the "miniaturization chamber." You're shrunk down to almost nothing and injected into a blood vessel in the patient's leg.

Now you find yourself at the submarine's main control panel. Your mission: to get to the patient's brain and fix the problem (in this case, superior cerebellar hemangioma) before an hour and ten minutes are up.

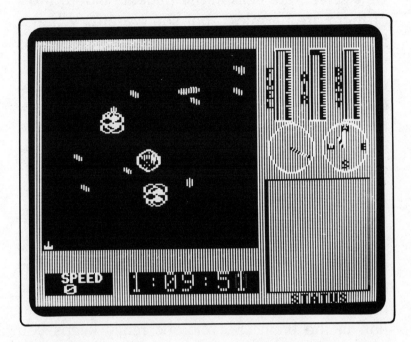

You're the captain of the sub; you pilot it and give all the orders. There are three other crew members: a navigator, who shows you maps of the body and helps steer the ship; a technician, who repairs any damage done to the ship; and a physician, who answers medical questions and recommends treatments.

In the upper right corner of the screen are the gauges that tell you how much fuel, air and electricity you have left. If you run out of air, the members of your crew pass out and then die. If you run out of fuel, you drift aimlessly along in a blood vessel, unable to control your sub.

Those cooties you see floating around in the big view screen are cells in the patient's blood. Most of them are harmless, but some aren't. When a hostile cell approaches, the sub's computer warns you. You quickly ask the physician to identify it, then recommend a treatment. The attackers all go by their correct medical names—giardia lamblia, herpes simplex virus, salmonella typhi, etc.—and so do the medicines you treat them with—metronidazole, acyclovir, ampicillin, and so on.

While all this is going on, you ask the physician for information on the patient's medical condition (you can even administer blood tests), tell the technician to repair damage to the ship caused by attackers that got through and, with the help of the navigator, guide the ship toward its final destination in the brain. So Microbe really keeps you hopping.

The program has some problems. The manual is confusing and doesn't tell you what you need to know, and the game is too hard at first— you're always dying before you get anywhere. But the basic idea is terrific, and Microbe is both educational and exciting.

Flight Simulator II

If you really like getting involved in what you're doing, you'll love Flight Simulator II (SubLOGIC).

It's such a realistic simulation that it comes with two manuals—one that tells you how to run the program and another that teaches you how to fly a plane (and these manuals are *terrific*— well organized, well written, and complete).

Flight Simulator II gives you a choice of flying in four parts of the country—Chicago, Los Angeles, Seattle and New York/Boston—and it provides you with realistic maps that show you the airports in all those areas. You can take off from one airport and land in another. Or you can just fly around and sightsee and then return home. You can do loops, rolls, Immelmans and other aerobatic stunts. (Personally, I like to crash the plane into buildings—when I can keep it in the air that long.)

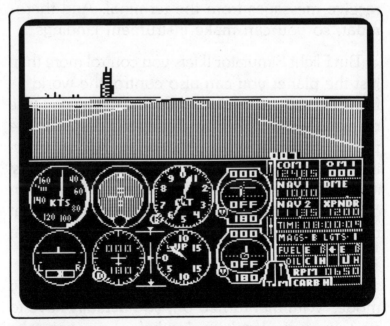

Flight Simulator on the ground at Meigs Field in Chicago

In the last screen, your plane is sitting on the runway at Meigs Field in Chicago, ready for takeoff. Flight Simulator II simulates an actual single-engine light plane—the Piper Archer II. As you can see, it does a pretty thorough job of recreating the cockpit—there are a lot of gauges and dials to pay attention to. But the instrument panel is just the beginning.

You have separate controls for the elevators, elevator trim, flaps, ailerons, rudder, throttle and brakes. You can thin out the fuel mixture, and you can switch from one fuel tank to the other (planes have one in each wing). You can look out the window in eight different directions (an improvement on a real plane). There's a radio on which you receive messages from the terminal. And there's radar, so you can make instrument landings.

But Flight Simulator II lets you control more than just the plane; you can also control the world it's flying in. You can decide what time of day you take off, what season it is, how cloudy it is, what altitude the clouds are at, what direction the wind is blowing from at three different altitudes, and how fast it's blowing at each of those altitudes. You can even control how reliable your plane is (from one that never has engine problems to one that has them often).

As if all that weren't enough, there's "reality mode." With that turned on, you actually have to start up your plane's engine before you can take off. Light bulbs in the instrument panel burn out.

And when night falls, the panel goes black—until you turn the lights on.

When you feel like you're getting pretty good at flying, you can choose "Europe 1917" and put yourself in the middle of World War I. Your mission is to take off from an airfield in friendly territory, fly over a river into enemy territory, and bomb their fuel depots and factories. There's just one slight hitch—the enemy has six fighters to defend these targets. So you get to practice your dog-fighting skills.

Now remember—this isn't just some stupid space-war arcade game. You're in a real plane (or something that behaves just like one). You have to actually *fly* it while all this is going on.

And that's the great thing about Flight Simulator II—it's so realistic, and so detailed, that after a few minutes you forget where you are and actually feel like you're flying. Unfortunately, there's no way to give you a sense of that with a few still pictures in a book. But take my word for it—Flight Simulator is an incredible simulation.

Since you can spend years flying a plane without getting tired of it, you can probably spend years with this program without getting tired of it. And that's a lot of value for $50.

Robot Odyssey

Robot Odyssey is a hot new game from the Learning Company. It builds on the same skills you learn in Rocky's Boots, but you don't have to have played that game to play this one.

The program has three parts. The first part is Robotropolis, an underground city populated by robots (you're the only human being there). Robotropolis has five levels: the sewer, the subway, the town, the master control center (the computer that runs Robotropolis) and the skyways (like streets, but in the air). You begin—you guessed it—in the sewer.

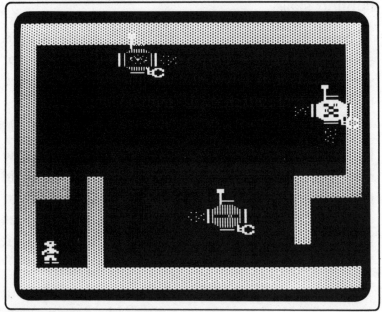

entering the sewer of Robotropolis

You find yourself in a room with three robots gliding aimlessly around, like fish in a fishbowl. You can move into the next room by yourself, but you'll find that you need a key to get any farther.

Since there's no key lying around anywhere you can see, there's only one place it could be—inside a robot. As you experiment, you'll find you can

the second room in the sewer of Robotropolis

get inside a robot just by walking in through one of its sides.

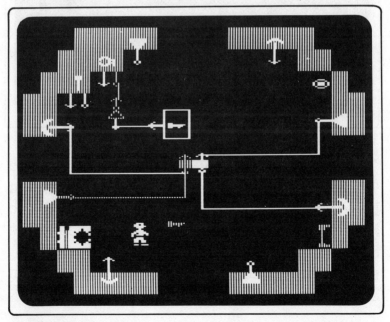

inside a robot

Now we're inside of one of the robots and, sure enough, the key is here. All these wires look pretty complicated, but Robot Odyssey contains three Robot Tutorials that teach you how robots work and how to build chips—electronic circuits shrunk down into tiny little packages— that make the robots do just about anything you want. These tutorials are a lot like the ones in Rocky's Boots, except they move faster and go farther.

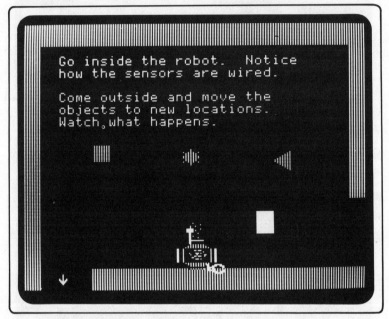

sample screen from a Robot Tutorial

Once you learn how chips are made, you go to the third part of Robot Odyssey, the Innovation Lab, to actually create some. The Innovation Lab has empty (unwired) robots, rooms full of parts (see the next illustration), and a maze to try out your newly-constructed chip in (you just pop it into an empty robot and test it).

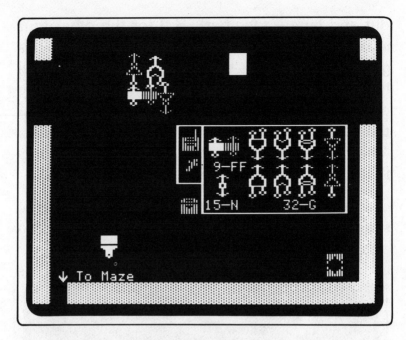

the parts room in the Innovation Lab

You can take the chips you make in the Innovation Lab back with you into Robotropolis, and, of course, that's one of the reasons you make them—to help you escape from Robotropolis (you can also build robots right in Robotropolis if you want). But there's another reason—the circuits in these chips are just like the circuits in real-life robots. What you learn about building them can all be applied to building actual robots. The Robot Odyssey manual even gives you the address of two robot-building clubs and a company that sells robot kits.

The manual also contains a map of the Robotropolis sewer (the map is three-dimensional and you have to make a copy of the page, cut it out and tape it together). But for the other four levels of Robotropolis, you're on your own. Things get more exciting as you move up from one level to the next (the main "street" of level 5 is really great). But even in the sewer there are "ampires" that suck electricity from your robots' batteries, "energy crystals" that recharge them, guard robots that keep you from getting to things, etc. etc.

Here's one of the sewers, filled with all kinds of strange creatures (that's you up on top, still holding onto the key):

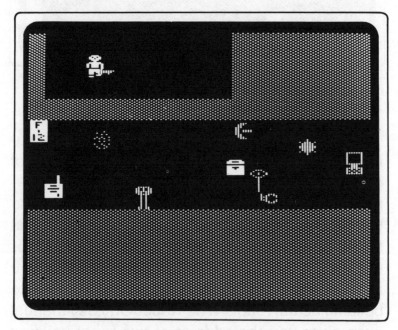

The great thing about Robot Odyssey is that it's really three great programs in one:

- Robotropolis is an exciting and interesting game of strategy and logic

- The Innovation Lab is an experimental workshop—sort of like a graphics program or a music program—where you futz around and create things (chips, in this case, instead of pictures or songs)

- The Robot Tutorials are a learning program which teaches you how to design electronic circuits just like the ones in real-life robots.

MindLink

MindLink is an incredible piece of equipment that was being developed by Atari before they almost went bankrupt, laid off almost everybody who worked for them, and got bought out by one of the founders of Commodore. When I was writing this book, it wasn't clear if MindLink was going to be put on the market or dumped by the new management. So I have no way of knowing if you'll even be able to buy it. But even if you can't, it's worth hearing about.

MindLink is a headband that can tell, from tiny little changes in the electricity that flows over your forehead, how relaxed you are (you didn't even know there was electricity flowing over your forehead, did you?). This information is transmitted by infrared waves (without wires) to the computer, where they can be used to control games. So you could have a car race where the more relaxed you are, the faster your car goes. You see your car going faster, you get excited...whoops! your car slows down.

Now that I've spent six chapters discussing all the wonderful programs other people have written, I'll tell you a little about how to write some of your own (in the next chapter).

Chapter 9

Programming a Computer (It's Easier than It Sounds)

A lot of people think that to use a computer, you have to learn how to program it. If you've read this far, you know that isn't true. But sometimes programs written by other people don't do exactly what you want them to do. That's one reason why you might want to do some programming of your own, but there are a couple of other reasons too.

One is that writing a best-selling piece of software is one of the fastest ways to make tons of money, and lots of software authors are in their teens (some are even younger). Of course 99% of all software doesn't earn peanuts, and programming well enough to write commercial software isn't easy.

Which brings us to the last reason for learning programming—it's fun. (You knew I was going to say that, didn't you?)

There are two ways to learn programming—you can pick a programming language to learn and jump right in, or you can start with one of several programs that teach you to think like a programmer without tying you down to a specific language. One of those is Pak Jana.

Pak Jana was a famous Indonesian dancer; that's him you see leaping around at the start of the chapter. You make Pak Jana dance by giving him programming **statements** (commands, instructions) like the ones printed on the screen next to him.

For example—there are six positions Pak Jana can hold his arms in, and the statements RIGHTARM 3, LEFTARM 1 tell him to put his right arm in position number 3 and his left arm in position number 1 (I told you programming wasn't hard). There are five positions for each leg, five ways his body can look, and ten different heads you can stick on him. He can jump up and down and move left and right.

To have even more fun, you can put several programming statements together—sort of like a little dance routine—and give them all one name. So let's do that. Here's Pak Jana just standing around waiting for us to tell him what to do:

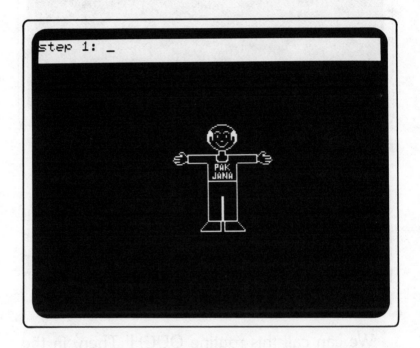

If we type LEFTLEG4 (or LL4—you're allowed to abbreviate) up at the top of the screen, he'll stick his left leg straight out. RL 4 will get him to do the same with his right. Now he's doing a split.

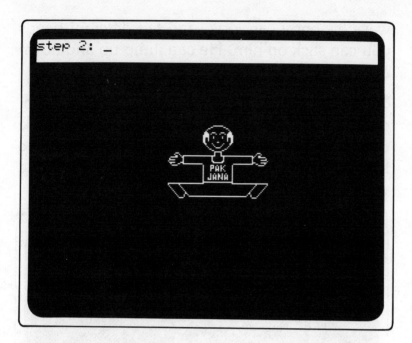

Pak Jana doing a split

But what if he were to fall down and land in this position? We can get him to move down the screen by typing DOWN 3. Now let's have him throw up his arms—LA (for "left arm") 2 and RA ("right arm") 2—and put on his saddest face—HEAD 10.

We can call this routine OUCH! Then, in the future, all anybody would have to do to make Pak Jana run through those six moves would be to type in OUCH! You can see how you could make up routines for Pak Jana that would get him to wave,

ouch!

jump, or even do a jig. And that, my friend, is basically all there is to programming.

Pak Jana is part of a software package called Mirrors on the Mind (published by Addison-Wesley) that approaches programming from several different angles. Another program in the package—Music Maker—teaches it through music; and two more—Keepers and Double Digit—teach it through gambling. There's even another dance program, called Annabel; it's similar to Pak Jana except that the dancer is a woman.

Spinnaker also has a program that teaches programming through drawing. It's called Delta Drawing and it gives you a powerful set of graphic commands; you can program some pretty impressive pictures with it.

Arrow Dynamics (published by Sunburst) teaches you basic programming concepts by having you play a strategy game that's a little like chess. The object of the game is to move an arrow across a game board. Ah, but you can't just move it; you have to *program* it to move. Once you know how to do that at the beginning level, you can add mirrors and other obstacles to make it harder for yourself.

As you can see, there are lots of ways to begin learning programming without having to study any particular language. But there's nothing wrong with using that approach either. Just as long as you don't study **BASIC**.

Many parents and teachers seem to think that the way to keep you out of the poorhouse when you grow up is to make sure you learn BASIC. Unfortunately, BASIC isn't going to do that. It was developed back in the mid-60's for use on computers that are primitive by today's standards. Although BASIC is very widely used today, it's on its way out.

And it deserves to be. It's a clumsy language and teaches you all kinds of bad programming habits. Alan Kay, one of the world's great computer geniuses, says that learning a little BASIC is not really going to give you any idea what programmers actually do, and that you'd get a better sense if you spent the same amount of time writing and producing plays (because plays give you a feeling for a lot of different forces interacting).

There are a lot of languages that are better than BASIC—Pascal, C, Modula 2, LISP, Forth, any assembly language. But everyone I've ever asked says there's really only one for a kid to begin with— **Logo**. Although Logo was developed specifically for kids, it's much more powerful than BASIC; in fact, it's closely related to LISP, the language used by people trying to teach computers to think like human beings (called **artificial intelligence**).

The basic level of Logo is **turtle graphics** (called that because it was originally taught using mechanical turtles that draw lines on paper). In turtle graphics, you use Logo commands to move a triangle around the screen that draws lines as it goes (it sounds stupid, but it's not).

You can buy the Logo language for just about any computer; for example, Apple sells a version for their machines. A good book about it is *Learning with Logo* (or *Learning with Apple Logo*) by Daniel Watt (McGraw-Hill). There's also a disk that works with the book, but it doesn't come with the book and—get this—you can't even buy it from McGraw-Hill. (For Apple Logo or Terrapin/Krell Logo, you order the disk from Creative Publications; for TI Logo, from Educational Alternatives.)

Logo Design Master (Koala) is a program that does a really neat thing. Normally, you come up with Logo programming statements and the turtle (the triangle on the screen) obeys them. With Logo Design Master, you draw the lines on a Koala Pad and the program shows them on the screen, figures out what programming statements would make those lines, and prints the statements out!

OK—in the next chapter I talk about what computers to buy, and what to look for when buying a piece of software.

Chapter 10

The Best Hardware and Software

This chapter assumes that you (or, more likely, your parents) can afford to buy some kind of computer hardware and software. If you can't, Chapter 12 tells you where you stand the best chance of getting your hands on some for free.

Hardware

No matter how good a machine is, if there aren't a lot of interesting programs written for it, you don't want to buy it. So first you decide what software you want to run, then you just find some hardware that will run that software.

Since it's hard to figure out in advance all the different programs you're ever going to want, the easiest approach is to buy the machine that has the largest total number of programs running on it. If you want to have access to the range of software I've been describing in this book, there are two brands to consider first—Apple and Commodore. (Most of the programs I've mentioned run on both of those machines, and almost all run on one or the other of them.)

the Commodore Model 16 computer

You can buy a Commodore Plus/4 or Model 16 (or a used Commodore 64 or PET) for a lot less than an Apple II, but you may wish you hadn't. The Commodore disk drive takes an *incredibly* long time to load a program into memory. Of course you can get around that by buying software on cartridges (since Commodores, unlike Apples, have a slot in the back for cartridges), but that really limits what you can get; most powerful software comes on disks.

If you can afford it, the Apple II is a better choice. I asked a number of people who know a lot about kids and computers what machine I should recommend to the readers of this book; every single one of them said "an Apple II." It's powerful enough for adults to do serious work on (and there's lots of good software to do that with, like AppleWorks and the PFS family), but it's also got tons of great games and learning programs. The Apple II will run

COURTESY OF COMMODORE BUSINESS MACHINES, INC.

the Commodore Plus/4 computer

10,000-20,000 programs, depending on the model. All in all, it's the ultimate machine for a family with kids (at least until there's more software for the Mac).

There have been four models of the Apple II so far. The first two are no longer made and can only be bought used. There's the original model, which is called simply the Apple II (it's also written "Apple][", but never "Apple 2"). This is an old-fashioned and primitive machine by today's standards, and you probably won't find many of them around.

The next model Apple made was the II+ (or][+)—a slightly jazzed-up version of the II. This is an OK machine, if you can get it at a decent price (it shouldn't cost much by now). But if you decide to buy a used machine (an Apple II, Commodore 64, Commodore PET, or whatever), be careful—it costs *at least* $50 an hour to get a computer repaired, and it can easily cost more to fix a used one than it would have cost to buy it new. Be sure you get some kind of warranty (at least 90 days parts and labor) on any used machine, and buy it from someone you trust.

The IIe (or //e) is a major improvement over the II and II+. It has a shift key that works the way it should (earlier models had to be rewired), so you can easily get lowercase letters. To get lines of 80 characters on the screen and 128K of memory, all you have to do is add one board. And it has many fewer chips in it, which means it runs cooler and is *even* more reliable than the earlier Apple II models.

Finally, there's the IIc (//c). This has to be one of the prettiest computers ever made, and it has

an Apple IIe with a unit that holds two disk drives

a lot of nice features—like 80-character lines and 128K of memory as standard equipment, and a disk drive built right into the side of the machine. It comes with four disks that teach you how to use it, and they are the best I've ever seen.

The IIc can run most of the software written for earlier Apple IIs, and many new programs for Apples will be written to take advantage of its expanded memory and other features. (There are some minor problems with it—the built-in disk drive could be sturdier, for example—but nothing serious.)

COURTESY OF APPLE COMPUTER, INC.

an Apple IIc with a mouse

If you can afford it, a IIe or a IIc is the machine to get. (The IIe will run more software and there's more equipment designed to plug right into it. The IIc is the more pleasant machine, both to look at and to work on.)

But can you afford it? All by itself, an Apple IIc is going to cost something like a thousand dollars, and that's only if you use a TV as a monitor (which is hard on the eyes) and don't buy a printer (which makes a serious dent in the fun you can have). A complete system—with a monitor, monitor stand, printer, joystick (or mouse), etc. will run quite a bit more than a thousand.

If you're going to do much graphics, you'll want a color monitor and a color printer; if you're going to do much word processing (or any other serious work), you'll want a second disk drive. Which means that a complete IIc system can easily cost between $2000 and $3000. A IIe will cost less, but it still won't be cheap.

A Commodore is much less expensive— although with a printer, monitor, etc., it can cost more than a thousand dollars too. But, according to one guy who knows a lot about home computers (I won't tell you his name, since his company makes products that work with many different kinds of machines and I'm sure he doesn't want to offend Commodore), people who spend less than $300 on a computer end up being terribly frustrated (he's talking about $300 just for the computer, that is— without a disk drive or anything else).

What it comes down to is this: If a Commodore is all you can afford, it's a *whole* lot better than nothing. But if you can afford an Apple, it's a whole lot better than a Commodore.

Of course it isn't just a question of what a computer costs. It's also a question of how adults decide what they can afford, and why they're willing to spend so much more money on useless junk than on computers. But that's a discussion I'll leave for the next chapter.

A third machine that may also be worth considering is the Atari 800XL. This is a great piece of hardware—it's fast and has graphics power that hasn't even been tapped yet. And there's a lot of good software that runs on it, including a word processing program— AtariWriter—that many people think is the best available for home computers.

So why didn't I put Atari up there with Apple and Commodore? Because it's not certain that either the company or its machines will be around for much longer, which makes people reluctant to write new software for it. Atari used to be one of the most famous makers of home computers, but then the people in charge made a lot of bad mistakes and the company almost went bankrupt. Now new people are in charge and Atari may be great again; if so, the Atari 800 series is definitely worth looking at.

Now—what if your parents already have an IBM Personal Computer (better known as a "PC") or one of the machines that imitates it (sometimes called "PC work-alikes" or "PC clones")? All is not lost. There are some good games that run on PCs, although there must be at least a hundred times as many on the Apple and Commodore.

Some PC clones have great graphics programs (although the PC itself doesn't). For things like word processing, keeping records, making graphs and the like, the PC software designed for adults will work fine for you. Unfortunately, software of all kinds tends to cost more on the PC than on an Apple or a Commodore.

The Macintosh (also made by Apple) is really a neat machine, and there will eventually be a lot of games and learning programs on it (there are already a fair number). As of right now, the Mac only has a black-and-white screen, but the image is really crisp and you can do *great* graphics on it. After you use a Mac for a little while, it's hard to go back to other computers. If your parents are thinking of buying a more expensive computer than an Apple IIc, try to steer them away from a PC and towards a Mac. It will be much more fun, for them as well as for you.

As I write this, in the fall of 1984, there's a rumor that Commodore is planning to bring out a color version of the Mac for under $1000! This seems incredible, but by the time you read this, it will either have happened or not. A color Mac for under a thousand dollars would obviously be a machine worth checking out. But pay attention to how much software is available for it (although if it's really as amazing as it sounds, a lot of people will be rushing to write programs for it).

Coleco is another manufacturer that used to sell a lot of home computers, but then they came out with a model that had a lot of things wrong with it, and you don't hear much about them any more.

As time goes on, there will probably be other home computers that give you a lot of machine for little money. Just remember—it's better to have a crummy, out-of-date machine that you can buy thousands of cheap programs for than an absolutely up-to-the-minute powerhouse that no one has written software for, or where every program costs a lot of money.

Software

There are more than 40,000 programs you can buy, and more than 6000 publishers selling them. Nine thousand of these programs are (supposed to be) educational. One group that evaluates software for schools (called EPIE) says that just *one* percent! of these are "exciting and use the full potential of the computers." So you can see that finding good software isn't going to be easy.

Hopefully this book has turned you on to some of the better software available. I don't have anything more to say about which specific programs are worth getting. But there are some general principles you can use (and get your parents and teachers to use) when evaluating software:

All software should be fun.

Regardless of what it's supposed to do, if it isn't any fun, it isn't any good. Unfortunately, most learning programs try to pound things into your skull with drill and practice. Aside from being boring, this isn't too smart—since just about nothing that can be taught by drill and practice is worth learning. (One exception is the alphabet—it does make sense to learn that by heart. There are a few others: the names of the numbers, the crazy way English words are spelled. But beyond stuff like that, drill and practice is a complete waste of the computer's capacity and your own.)

Unfortunately, some "educators" don't realize that. They can't think very clearly, and they certainly don't want you thinking any more clearly than they. So they try to cram you full of things like the names of all the states' capitals, or all the presidents.

You'd be amazed how handy that kind of information can be in everyday life. Once in a job interview I was asked if I knew who was president between Millard Fillmore and James Buchanan, and what the capital of Missouri is; if I hadn't known the answers (Ronald Reagan and Katmandu), I probably wouldn't have gotten the job.

Albert Einstein once told an interviewer that he didn't know the speed of sound (a pretty basic fact for a physicist). When the reporter was surprised, and asked him why not, Einstein said, "Why should I clutter up my head with things I can look up in a book?"

A few years before the big student revolt in Paris in 1968, the national student association put out a poster that had the right attitude toward mindless memorization. The caption read, "No more cram-ming. Let students participate in their education." The educational authorities paid no attention (of course), and eventually the students rebelled.

from a French student poster (1964)

What education should do—and what computers should do—is help you *think* better. Teachers and school administrators who waste your time—and a computer's power—on drill and practice should have a bunch of dental students drill and practice on them.

Memorization isn't the only thing that can make software boring. Some programs seem like fun at first, but there's so little to them that you soon get bored with them (this is true of a lot of arcade-style action games). Good software is interesting at first, and *stays* interesting for a long time.

(By the way, there's a computer slang term for what I've just been doing. It's called "flaming on" and it means you go on raving endlessly about something. If you like what someone is saying when they're ranting like this, you say, "All right! Flame on!")

Good software is easy to learn and easy to use.

Life is too short to hassle with the results of other people's laziness. You pay good money for a program, and you shouldn't end up lost and wondering what to do. If a program makes you feel stupid, it's not because you are; it's because the person who wrote the program is.

A good manual and a good reference card can both help make a program easy to learn—although with some programs you really don't need either of them.

Good support is part of a good program.

No matter how well a program is thought out, things can go wrong. And if they do, you want someone you can turn to with your questions. You pay less for software at a discount store or by mail order than if you buy it from a computer store, but you don't have anybody local to turn to if a problem arises.

If the publisher is good enough, though, this won't matter. Sunburst, for example, puts a (toll-free) 800 number right on the label of all their disks. If you have a question or a problem, you just call them up.

If a company puts out one good program, they're likely to put out other good ones.

So, for example, The Learning Company, which publishes two of the best programs ever written (Rocky's Boots and Robot Odyssey), also has a whole bunch of other great programs (I haven't mentioned them only because they're for younger kids). Some other companies that I'd expect to bring out good software most of the time are: Scarborough, Koala, Broderbund and Apple.

This principle also works for smaller, more specialized companies. For example, I wouldn't necessarily depend on Sir-Tech to bring out a good music program, but I'd bet that any role-playing games they bring out will be terrific. (I'm waiting for the Macintosh version of Wizardry myself.)

Actually, the easiest way to predict if a program is going to be any good is to know who wrote it. For example, you can depend on Bill Atkinson never to write a bad graphics program, on Bill Finzer never to write a bad learning program, and so on. Unfortunately, only a few programs have the author's name on the package. Hopefully this will change, and software will become more like books, where when you read one you like, it's easy to find others written by the same person.

(Tom Snyder is one author of games whose name regularly appears on the outside of the package, so if you like Snooper Troops and In Search of the Most Amazing Thing, you can look for others by him.)

Finally, it's nice to have good packaging.

Here's what I think makes up a good package:

- It should open like a book, and there should be a pocket inside to hold the disk against some hard surface (if there is no hard surface, or if the disk is loose inside the package, there's a good chance it will get bent out of shape and destroyed).

- You shouldn't have to take the manual out of a pocket to read it; it should be attached to the package so you can leaf through it without removing it.

- The package shouldn't be made of some horrible smelly vinyl that makes you sick and gives you cancer. If it is plastic, at least it should be the kind that doesn't smell too bad.

- It should be pretty. After all, if the program's any good, it's going to be around for a while; why shouldn't it be a pleasure to look at? My personal favorites for pretty packages are those from Spinnaker, Apple, The Learning Company and Electronic Arts.

Well, campers, that's about it. Now that you know what the best hardware and software to buy are, it's time to find out how to trick...I mean, how to persuade your parents and teachers to buy them for you. That's what the next chapter is about.

Chapter 11

Getting Parents and Teachers to Buy the Right Stuff

I have a friend who needs a computer to run his business, whose wife needs it to do architectural designs, and whose kids need it for a whole bunch of things—games, learning programs, writing reports for school, and so on. The only one in the family who doesn't need a computer is the dog.

Even though my friend has a lot of money, he's

hesitated about buying a computer for years. He's afraid he'll end up spending a few hundred dollars more than he should, or that he'll get a system that isn't absolutely the most perfect one possible. And yet this same guy doesn't think twice about buying an old car, spending $20,000 (and hundreds of hours of his own time) fixing it up, and then—when he's finally got it in absolutely mint condition—selling it for $10,000.

Well, my friend is obviously nuts, but a lot of grownups are the same way. They'll spend a small fortune redecorating their living rooms, or buying an "option package" for their car that amounts to a bunch of chrome, a few decals, and some other junk. But when it comes to buying a computer, they pinch every quarter till the eagle screams.

That's really sad, because computers deliver more value, more satisfaction, more enjoyment per dollar than just about anything else you can buy. I've spent much more on computer equipment than on my car, and I'll continue to do that, even though my car is an old rattletrap people laugh at (except for the foam dice hanging from the rearview mirror—everybody loves the foam dice). If someone gave me an extra thousand dollars today, you can bet I'd spend it on computers, not on my living room.

If your parents really understood how much fun a computer can be, and how much you can learn from it, they'd be willing to spend a lot more money on one (unless, of course, they really can't afford to spend anything; in that case, see Chapter 12).

But even when adults are willing to set aside a reasonable amount of money for computer hardware and software, they usually have no idea what to buy—or, worse, they know exactly what to buy, and they're dead wrong.

So it's your job to educate them, using this book as ammunition. (If you think your parents won't like my style, or that they'll want to hear the same thing from two different sources, there's a good book aimed specifically at parents. It's called *Parents, Kids, and Computers* and was written by my friends Lynne Alper and Meg Holmberg (and published by Sybex). Lynne and Meg's book isn't as hard-nosed as mine on a number of points (which may appeal to your parents more), but we agree on everything major.

Even without that book, there's certainly enough evidence in this one, scattered throughout the pages. But facts alone aren't enough. Since you're not dealing with totally rational creatures, you'll need to use a little adult psychology.

The basic principles of adult psychology

The most important thing to remember about adults is how insecure they are. That's understandable—they have a lot to worry about. They know how hard it's been for them to make a living, and how expensive everything is (they've spent a fortune on you so far, and look what they've got to show for it). So naturally they worry about how you're going to get by when you grow up.

Now you and I both know that the best possible preparation for the world is to let your mind and imagination develop to their fullest. And it's obvious from what you've been reading here that computers are a great tool for doing that.

But your parents are being told that if you don't learn to program in BASIC (or memorize all the state capitals), you'll end up on a street corner selling pencils. When you come to them all enthusiastic about this computer stuff, they think, "Well, sure, it's exciting, but is it what my kid *needs?*"

So, you have to convince them—not that you'd *enjoy* this "game" more than that "learning program"—but that the game will teach you more important things, and that what you learn from it will help you succeed when you're grown up. You don't do that jumping up and down and whining; you do it by patiently proving to them (this might take months) that:

- *all* good software, regardless of its purpose, is *fun*
- you learn more when you're having fun.

One good argument you can use is that all the real computer hot shots were people who went off on their own and did what they felt like doing because it was fun. In other words, they didn't study computers—they futzed around with them. That's how Steve Wozniak and Steve Jobs designed the first Apple computer. That's how Bill Gates wrote the first computer language that ran on small computers; in fact, he dropped out of Harvard to do it. I could give you fifty more examples.

If your parents are serious about wanting you to make it in the computer field, they'll let you follow your instincts and do what you enjoy. There are going to be fewer and fewer good jobs in the future, and the people who get them are going to be unusual, not ordinary.

(By the way, computers are one field where women can really get ahead. I've already mentioned the fabulous Ada Lovelace; another woman computer pioneer is Grace Hopper, who developed a famous computer language called COBOL.)

Educating teachers

The main thing to understand about teachers is how overloaded they are, and how much nonsense they have to put up with from school administrators. Because they're being hassled from every side, they don't have a lot of time to study computer products, and they have to rely on what other people tell them. Sometimes the advice they get is good; often it's not.

Your school may have a teacher who's a specialist in computer education, and s/he's more likely to know what's good. If not, recommend an organization called EPIE (Educational Products Information Exchange; their address is listed in the appendix). EPIE studies learning programs and reports on them.

Another organization that knows a lot about the best learning programs, particularly in math and science, is called EQUALS in Computer Technology (its address and phone number are listed in the appendix). EQUALS is dedicated to getting more girls and minority kids involved in science, mathematics and computers, and in the process of doing that, they learned a *lot* about computer software in general. They give workshops for teachers and publish booklets, and they really know their stuff.

You don't have to be a computer specialist to take advantage of EQUALS (or EPIE either); any teacher or school can use their services.

But even with good organizations like this, you can't leave the education of your teachers entirely in other people's hands; you have to take some responsibility for it yourself. Recommend some of the programs mentioned in this book, and show your teachers what I say about them. Prepare a written report on worthwhile computer products; you could even make it a review of this book. The more you present your ideas in the way teachers like—neat, well-organized, to the point—the more attention they're going to pay to what you say.

Although most of the programs I've talked about in this book are designed basically for home use, they'd all work well in a classroom too. But there are a couple of good programs I haven't talked about yet, because they're really designed mostly for school use. One of them is called Simpolicon (Cross Cultural Software).

Simpolicon is a game that simulates the economic development of countries. Each country has six interest groups—agriculture, business, consumer protection, health, education and the military, and each of these interest groups wants the country to develop in a different way. The educators want to build more schools, the farmers want to grow more food, the military wants to train more soldiers, and so on.

Before you start playing, the interest groups argue it out and decide on a set of goals for your nation as a whole. (Usually one or more students represent each group. If you're playing alone, you just do the arguing in your head). The play is divided into "years," and you can play for as many years as you like, changing your goals after each one.

There are 63 products you can make—everything from rice to steel to agricultural equipment to health clinics to land beautification—and at the end of each "year," Simpolicon puts it all together and tells you how the country is doing. But it's not as simple as that. There can be natural disasters (like hurricanes or floods), or your country can be invaded by another; the chance of these things happening increases every year. Also, your population can grow, giving you more mouths to feed.

Simpolicon's year-end summary tells you a lot of different things:

- It adds up all that you've produced during the year.

- It calculates your country's gross national product (the total value of everything you've produced during the year) and your national wealth (the total value of everything in your country).

- It reports on how much you have left of several natural resources—farming land, grazing land, forests, oil, coal, gold and half a dozen other minerals—and what kinds of jobs the people in your country have.

- It tells you what the "quality of life" is like in your country—how many schools, hospitals and "cultural facilities" (movie theatres, museums, etc.) there are, how many deaths there were, how pretty the land is, how much pollution there is.

- It reports on how each special interest group did in terms of its own goals.

- Finally, it puts everything together and

gives your country a score (based on its stated goals) for that year.

Simpolicon will let you have up to thirty separate countries on each disk, and there are several different ways the game can be played. One single student can be a country and play the game alone. Two students can each be a country and play against each other. A small group of four to eight students can make up one country, with four or five countries in the classroom making up a simulated world. Or each class of students can become one or two countries, with the whole school becoming the world and countries from different classrooms engaging in "international trade."

The man who wrote Simpolicon is a high-school teacher who spent ten years of his life developing it. He and many other teachers have used it with great success in junior high and high school classes. The kids love playing it, and in at least one class, that's all they did for a whole semester.

In a letter I wrote to Simpolicon's author, I said: "Social studies teachers could hardly do better by their classes than to have them simply play Simpolicon for a semester or a year—both from the point of view of how much the students would learn, and also how involved they'd become in their learning. I predict that Simpolicon will become a classic." On top of all that, Simpolicon is very inexpensive.

There's also a home version of Simpolicon, by

the way, in case you get really hooked on it, or in case you can't convince your teacher to buy it, and it's even cheaper than the school version. One possible hangup: Simpolicon requires an Apple II with two disk drives.

Another good school program is Math Worlds (Sterling Swift). Written by the same people who wrote Mirrors on the Mind, Math Worlds lets you set up your own simulated businesses, decide when a television network should schedule different programs, figure out who populates a make-believe planet, come up with strategies for winning an ancient game called Nim, and so on. While you're doing all this, you're learning important concepts like symmetry, sampling, probability and inference.

Well, that just about covers it. Good luck with your parents and teachers.

The next chapter tells you where to get more information about computers, including how to find ones you can use for free.

Chapter 12

Where to Get More Information about Computers, and How to Use One for Free if You Can't Afford to Buy One

There are a number of good magazines about computers written for kids. One of the best is called *Enter*; it's published by the Children's Television Workshop (the people who bring you Sesame Street) and its address is in the appendix.

But there's no reason you can't read adult computer magazines too, as long as you stay away from the very technical ones like *BYTE*. There are magazines about Apple, Atari and Commodore computers, and some good general ones too. *Consumer Reports* sometimes has good articles on home computers; you can find it in most libraries. Before deciding to subscribe to any magazine, be sure to buy a copy of it at a newsstand to see what it's like.

A wonderful place to find things out is at a **user group**. This is a bunch of people who get together regularly to talk about their computers and what they're doing with them. Usually a user group is specific to one computer, so it'll be called the Commodore User Group of Toledo, the Twin Cities Apple User Group, or something like that.

User groups are great places to get information, since almost all the people who go are enthusiastic about their computers, probably spend a lot of time with them, and almost certainly know a lot about them. Also—unlike the salesmen in computer stores (who are trying to sell you something—that's their job, after all) or the people who write articles in computer magazines (who have to be careful not to offend the magazine's advertisers)—the people at user group meetings have no reason not to tell you just exactly what they think.

Getting free use of a computer can be fairly hard or fairly easy, depending on where you live. Here are a few ways you can go about it:

- Go to a lot of user group meetings and make friends with some of the people there. They'll probably enjoy showing you things on their computers and, if you get to be good friends, will probably let you use them by yourself some of the time.

- Call your local library and ask if they have any computer facilities that the public can use. This is a long shot, but it's worth a phone call. As software gets more and more common, the pressure on libraries to provide some place where you can try it out will increase.

- If there's a science museum near you, call them and see if they have computer classes you can take and/or computer equipment you can use. Most of them do, and the ones that don't should be ashamed of themselves. (This won't be free, but it will be cheap.) Look in the Yellow Pages under "Museums" and try any that seem likely.

- Do the same thing for your local school district and for neighboring school districts. Often they have places where teachers can go look at software and you might be able to sweet-talk them into letting you pay a visit. Or some neighboring school might have computer classes you could wangle your way into (I'm assuming, of course, that you'll try to get into any computer classes in your own school.

Remember—first impressions are important. If you can convince an adult that you're a bright, serious kid who's being deprived of all the wonderful educational experiences a computer can provide just because your family is too poor to afford one, they will go out of their way (and bend rules) to help you.

- Here's a general rule that you'll find useful in lots of different situations: *Whenever* anyone tells you that they're sorry but they can't help you, ask them if they have any idea where you might find what you're looking for.

Say Ms. Stubbs at the library suggests that you call her friend Ms. Zarifa at the school district. Whenever you have a specific person's name, be sure to use the name of the person who gave it to you right at the start of the phone conversation, like this: "Hello, Ms. Zarifa? Ms. Stubbs at the library suggested I give you a call. I'm trying to find a place where I can use a computer..."

Well, pardner, that ol' sun is startin' to set over the prairie and it's time for your ol' Uncle Arthur and his faithful horse Melvin to be headin' down that ol' lonesome trail. It's sure been swell chewin' the fat with you...Now wipe that tear from your eye! You got no call to be carrying on like that...Like I was saying, It's sure been swell chewin' the fat with you, little pardner, and I hope we can do it again sometime.

Appendix

Addresses and phone numbers of companies
who make products mentioned in the book

Addison-Wesley
225 Sand Hill Road
Menlo Park CA 94025
415/ 854-0300
    Annabel
    Double Digit
    Keepers
    Music Maker
    Pak Jana

Apple Computer
20525 Mariani Avenue
Cupertino CA 95014
800/ 662-9238
    Apple II
    Apple IIc
    Apple IIe
    Apple II+
    The AppleWorks Data Base
    The AppleWorks
      Spreadsheet
    The AppleWorks Word
      Processor

Atari
1265 Borregas Avenue
Sunnyvale CA 94086
408/ 745-2000
    Atari 800 XL
    AtariWriter

Broderbund
17 Paul Drive
San Rafael CA 94903
415/ 479-1170
    Bank Street Speller
    Bank Street Writer
    The Print Shop

Chalk Board
3772 Pleasantdale Road
Atlanta GA 30340
404/ 447-6711
    PowerPad

The Children's Television
    Workshop
1 Lincoln Plaza
New York NY 10023
212/ 595-3456
    Enter Magazine

City Software
735 West Wisconsin Avenue
Milwaukee WI 53233
414/ 291-5125
    Doodle!

Coleco Industries
23 Chelton Avenue
West Hartford CT 06110
800/ 842-1225

Commodore
1200 Wilson Drive
West Chester PA 19380
215/ 431-9100
    Commodore Model 16
    Commodore Pet
    Commodore Plus/4
    Commodore 64

Computer Colorworks
3030 Bridgeway
Sausalito CA 94965
415/ 331-3022
    Flying Colors

Consumer Reports
256 Washington Street
Mount Vernon NY 10553

Creative Publications
Box 10328
Palo Alto CA 94303
415/ 968-3977
  Apple Logo Procedures Disk
  Terrapin/Krell Logo
    Procedures Disk

Cross Cultural Software
5385 Elrose Avenue
San Jose CA 95124
408/ 267-1044
  Simpolicon

Designware
Suite 158, Building 3
185 Berry Street
San Francisco CA 94701
415/ 546-1866
  Spellicopter
  Crypto Cube

Educational Alternatives
Gregg Lake Road
Antrim NH 03440
  TI Logo Procedures Disk

EPIE
(Educational Products
  Information Exchange)
Box 839
Water Mill NY 11976
516/ 283-4922

Electronic Arts
2755 Campus Drive
San Mateo CA 94403
415/ 571-7171
  Music Construction Set
  Pinball Construction Set

Equals in Computer
Technology
Lawrence Hall of Science
University of California
Berkeley CA 94720
415/ 642-1823

Hayden Software Company
600 Suffolk Street
Lowell MA 01853
800/ 343-1218
  PIE Writer
  The Speller
  The Writer

IBM
Box 1328
Boca Raton FL 33432
800/ 447-4700
  IBM Personal Computer

Infocom
55 Wheeler Street
Cambridge MA 02138
617/ 492-1031
  Zork III

Kaypro
533 Stevens Avenue
Solana Beach CA 94075
619/ 481-4300
  Kaypro computers

Koala Technologies
3100 Patrick Henry Drive
Santa Clara CA 95052
408/ 986-8866
  Koala Pad
  KoalaPainter
  Logo Design Master

L & S Computerware
1008 Stewart Drive
Sunnyvale CA 94086
408/ 738-3416
  Crossword Magic

The Learning Company
Suite 170, 545 Middlefield
Road
Menlo Park CA 94025
415/ 328-5410
  Rocky's Boots
  Robot Odyssey

Milliken Publishing
1100 Research Boulevard
St. Louis MO 63132
  The Milliken Word Processor

Reston Publishing
11480 Sunset Hills Road
Reston VA 22090
800/ 336-0338
  Paint

Scarborough Systems
25 North Broadway
Tarrytown NY 10591
914/ 332-4545
  MasterType
  Phi Beta Filer
  PictureWriter
  SongWriter

Sierra On-Line
Coarsegold CA 93614
209/ 683-6858
  Homeword

Sir-Tech Software
6 Main Street
Ogdensburg NY 13669
315/ 393-6633
  Wizardry

Software Publishing
1901 Landings Drive
Mountain View CA 94043
415/ 962-0191
  PFS:Access
  PFS:File
  PFS:Graph
  PFS:Proof
  PFS:Write

Spinnaker Software
One Kendell Square
Cambridge MA 02139
617/ 494-1200
  Delta Drawing
  In Search of the Most
  Amazing Thing
  Snooper Troops

Sterling Swift Publishing
7901 South IH-35
Austin TX 78744
512/ 282-6840
  Math Worlds

SubLOGIC
13 Edgebrook Drive
Champaign IL 61820
217/ 359-8482
  Flight Simulator II

Sunburst Communications
39 Washington Avenue
Pleasantville NY 10570
800/ 431-1934
  Arrow Dynamics
  Code Quest
  The Factory
  Fun House Maze
  The Incredible Laboratory
  The King's Rule

Sybex
2344 Sixth Street
Berkeley CA 94710
415/ 848-8233
  Parents, Kids, and
  Computers

Synergistic Software
Suite 201, 830 North Riverside
Drive
Renton WA 98055
206/ 226-3216
  Microbe

Index